9

STUDY GUIDE

Dictatorship and Conflict in the USSR, 1924–53

Edexcel - IGCSE

app
available

Published by Clever Lili Limited.

contact@cleverlili.com

First published 2020

ISBN 978-1-913887-08-7

Contributors: Lynn Harkin, Jonathan Boyd, Megan Quirk

Edited by Paul Connolly and Rebecca Parsley

Design by Evgeni Veskov and Will Fox

DISCOVER MORE OF OUR IGCSE HISTORY STUDY GUIDES

GCSEHistory.com and Clever Lili

Edexcel - IGCSE

STUDY GUIDE

Germany: Development of Dictatorship, 1918–45

GCSEHistory.com

Edexcel - IGCSE

STUDY GUIDE

A World Divided: Superpower Relations, 1943–72

GCSEHistory.com

Edexcel - IGCSE

STUDY GUIDE

Russia and the Soviet Union, 1905–24

GCSEHistory.com

Edexcel - IGCSE

STUDY GUIDE

The Origins and Course of the First World War, 1905–18

GCSEHistory.com

Edexcel - IGCSE

STUDY GUIDE

The Vietnam Conflict, 1945–75

GCSEHistory.com

Edexcel - IGCSE

STUDY GUIDE

A Divided Union: Civil Rights in the USA, 1945–74

GCSEHistory.com

Edexcel - IGCSE

STUDY GUIDE

The USA, 1918–41

GCSEHistory.com

Edexcel - IGCSE

STUDY GUIDE

Changes in Medicine, c1848–c1948

GCSEHistory.com

Edexcel - IGCSE

STUDY GUIDE

China: Conflict, Crisis and Change, 1900–89

GCSEHistory.com

THE GUIDES ARE EVEN BETTER WITH OUR GCSE/IGCSE HISTORY WEBSITE APP AND MOBILE APP

GCSE History is a text and voice web and mobile app that allows you to easily revise for your GCSE/IGCSE exams wherever you are - it's like having your own personal GCSE history tutor. Whether you're at home or on the bus, GCSE History provides you with thousands of convenient bite-sized facts to help you pass your exams with flying colours. We cover all topics - with more than 120,000 questions - across the Edexcel, AQA and CIE exam boards.

GCSEHistory.com

GET IT ON
Google Play

Download on the
App Store

Contents

How to use this book.. 5

What is this book about? 6

Revision suggestions 8

Timelines

Dictatorship and Conflict in the USSR, 1924 to 1953................................... 12

Leadership Struggle, 1924 - 1929

Contenders in The Leadership Struggle, 1924-1929 14

How Stalin won the Leadership Struggle, 1924-1929 16

Economic Policies, 1921 - 1941

New Economic Policy, 1921-1928 18

Industrialisation.. 20

Five Year Plans 22

Gosplan 23

First Five Year Plan, 1928-32 24

Second Five Year Plan, 1933-37 25

Third Five Year Plan, 1938-41 26

The Stakhanovite Movement 26

Collectivisation, 1930s.. 27

Kulaks 30

Controlling the People: Terror and Purges

The Purges, 1930-1953 31

The Secret Police.. 34

The Gulags 35

Controlling the People: Censorship and Propaganda

Stalin's Cult of Personality 37

Soviet Propaganda under Stalin 38

Soviet Censorship under Stalin 38

Socialist Realism 39

1936 Constitution 40

Life in the Soviet Union, 1924 - 1941

Living in Towns and the Countryside, 1924-41...................... 41

Working in Towns and the Countryside, 1924-41 42

Family Life, 1924-41... 43

Changes in Society, 1917 - 1941

Communist Policies on Women, 1924-1941 44

Communist Policies on Education, 1924-1941 46

Communist Policies on Family, 1924-1941.......................... 47

Communist Policies on Art and Culture, 1924-1941 48

Communist Policies on Religion, 1924-1941........................ 49

Stalin's Great Retreat... 50

Ethnic Groups 51

The Second World War

The Nazi-Soviet Pact, 1939 52

The Nazi Invasion of the USSR, 1941 53

Stalin's Leadership 55

The Battle of Stalingrad, 1942 56

The Soviet Invasion of Germany 57

The Impact of the Second World War on the USSR 58

Post-Second World War, 1945 - 1953

Fourth Five Year Plan, 1946 to 1950............................... 59

Stalin's Legacy.. 60

People of the USSR

Lev Kamenev 60

Sergei Kirov 61

Vladimir Lenin 61

Joseph Stalin 62

Leon Trotsky 63

Genrikh Yagoda - NKVD... 63

Nikolai Yezhov - NKVD 63

Grigory Zinoviev 63

Glossary.. 7

Index 7

In this study guide, you will see a series of icons, highlighted words and page references. The key below will help you quickly establish what these mean and where to go for more information.

Icons

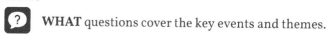 **WHAT** questions cover the key events and themes.

WHO questions cover the key people involved.

WHEN questions cover the timings of key events.

WHERE questions cover the locations of key moments.

WHY questions cover the reasons behind key events.

HOW questions take a closer look at the way in which events, situations and trends occur.

IMPORTANCE questions take a closer look at the significance of events, situations, and recurrent trends and themes.

DECISIONS questions take a closer look at choices made at events and situations during this era.

Highlighted words

Abdicate - occasionally, you will see certain words highlighted within an answer. This means that, if you need it, you'll find an explanation of the word or phrase in the glossary which starts on **page 71**.

Page references

Tudor *(p. 7)* - occasionally, a certain subject within an answer is covered in more depth on a different page. If you'd like to learn more about it, you can go directly to the page indicated.

Dictatorship and conflict in the USSR, 1924-53 is the historical investigation that studies how and why Stalin transformed the USSR between 1924 and 1953. You will focus on crucial events during this period, and study the different social, cultural, political, economic, military and religious changes that occurred.

Purpose

This study will help you to understand the nature of dictatorship. You will investigate themes such as power, law and order, government, censorship, propaganda, art and culture, communism, dictatorship, economy and society. This course will enable you to develop the historical skills of analysing and evaluating historical interpretations. You will also develop the skills of explaining, analysing and making judgements about events. You will use the concepts of cause, consequences, change, continuity, similarity, difference and significance.

Topics

Dictatorship and conflict in the USSR, 1924-53 is split into 5 key enquiries:

- Enquiry 1 looks at the leadership struggle between 1924 and 1929. You will study how and why Stalin succeeded in the leadership struggle after Lenin's death. You will investigate the reasons for Stalin's success and the failures of his rivals.

- Enquiry 2 looks at Stalin's Five Year Plans and collectivisation. You will investigate the reasons for the introduction of the Five Year Plans, their aims, and their successes and failures. You will also study the policy of collectivisation; its causes, nature and consequences.

- Enquiry 3 looks at purges, show trials, the cult of Stalin and the revision of history. You will study the reasons for the purges, what happened and the impact on the USSR, as well as the role of individuals involved. You will also investigate how Stalin used his cult of personality to control the people.

- Enquiry 4 looks at life in the USSR between 1924 and 1941. You will study the effects of the government's policies on women, families and ethnic groups. You will explore the differences between the towns and the countryside.

- Enquiry 5 looks at the Second World War and after, between 1941 and 1953. You will study how the USSR fared in the war and the significance of the Battle of Stalingrad. You will investigate the final years of Stalin in terms of the post-war purges, the Fourth Five Year Plan and the impact of his declining health on his power.

Key Individuals

Some of the key individuals studied on this course include:

- Joseph Stalin.
- Leon Trotsky.
- Nikolai Bukharin.
- Lev Kamenev.
- Grigory Zinoviev.
- Genrikh Yagoda.
- Nikolai Yezhov.

Key Events

Some of the key events you will study on this course include:

- The leadership struggle between 1924 and 1929.
- First Five Year Plan and collectivisation.
- Murder of Kirov.
- The Great Purge and the show trials.
- Nazi Germany invasion of the USSR in Operation Barbarossa.
- Socialist Realism in art and culture.
- Stalin's Great Retreat in education.

Assessment

Dictatorship and conflict in the USSR, 1924-53 forms part of paper 1 where you have a total of 1 hour and 30 minutes to complete. You should spend 45 minutes on this section of the paper. There will be 1 exam question on Dictatorship and conflict in the USSR, 1924-53. The question will be broken down into 4 sections; a, b, c(i) and c(ii). You will answer a, b and either c(i) or c(ii).

Question a is worth 6 marks. This question will require you to examine an extract and assesses your ability to analyse and evaluate a historical interpretation. You will need to identify the author's opinion or perspective by analysing the language the author uses and what they have chosen to comment on. You will explain how valid the overall interpretation is by using your own knowledge to evaluate the interpretation.

Question b is worth 6 marks. This question will require you to explain two effects of an event on something else by using your contextual knowledge and looking at the consequences. You will need to identify two effects and then demonstrate how the event led to the effect you have identified.

Question c(i) and c(ii) are worth 16 marked. This question will require you to construct an argument to support and challenge an interpretation stated in the question. You will be given two pieces of information to help jog your memory but you must use information of your own. You will have the opportunity to show your ability to explain and analyse historical events using 2nd order concepts such as causation, consequence, change, continuity, similarity and difference.

Revision! A dreaded word. Everyone knows it's coming, everyone knows how much it helps with your exam performance, and everyone struggles to get started! We know you want to do the best you can in your IGCSEs, but schools aren't always clear on the best way to revise. This can leave students wondering:

- ✓ How should I plan my revision time?
- ✓ How can I beat procrastination?
- ✓ What methods should I use? Flash cards? Re-reading my notes? Highlighting?

Luckily, you no longer need to guess at the answers. Education researchers have looked at all the available revision studies, and the jury is in. They've come up with some key pointers on the best ways to revise, as well as some thoughts on popular revision methods that aren't so helpful. The next few pages will help you understand what we know about the best revision methods.

How can I beat procrastination?

This is an age-old question, and it applies to adults as well! Have a look at our top three tips below.

◎ Reward yourself

When we think a task we have to do is going to be boring, hard or uncomfortable, we often put if off and do something more 'fun' instead. But we often don't really enjoy the 'fun' activity because we feel guilty about avoiding what we should be doing. Instead, get your work done and promise yourself a reward after you complete it. Whatever treat you choose will seem all the sweeter, and you'll feel proud for doing something you found difficult. Just do it!

◎ Just do it!

We tend to procrastinate when we think the task we have to do is going to be difficult or dull. The funny thing is, the most uncomfortable part is usually making ourselves sit down and start it in the first place. Once you begin, it's usually not nearly as bad as you anticipated.

◎ Pomodoro technique

The pomodoro technique helps you trick your brain by telling it you only have to focus for a short time. Set a timer for 20 minutes and focus that whole period on your revision. Turn off your phone, clear your desk, and work. At the end of the 20 minutes, you get to take a break for five. Then, do another 20 minutes. You'll usually find your rhythm and it becomes easier to carry on because it's only for a short, defined chunk of time.

◎ Spaced practice

We tend to arrange our revision into big blocks. For example, you might tell yourself: "This week I'll do all my revision for the Cold War, then next week I'll do the Medicine Through Time unit."

This is called **massed practice**, because all revision for a single topic is done as one big mass.

But there's a better way! Try **spaced practice** instead. Instead of putting all revision sessions for one topic into a single block, space them out. See the example below for how it works.

This means planning ahead, rather than leaving revision to the last minute - but the evidence strongly suggests it's worth it. You'll remember much more from your revision if you use **spaced practice** rather than organising it into big blocks. Whichever method you choose, though, remember to reward yourself with breaks.

Spaced practice (more effective):

week 1	week 2	week 3	week 4
Topic 1	Topic 1	Topic 1	Topic 1
Topic 2	Topic 2	Topic 2	Topic 2
Topic 3	Topic 3	Topic 3	Topic 3
Topic 4	Topic 4	Topic 4	Topic 4

Massed practice (less effective)

week 1	week 2	week 3	week 4
Topic 1	Topic 2	Topic 3	Topic 4

What methods should I use to revise?

Self-testing/flash cards

Self explanation/mind-mapping

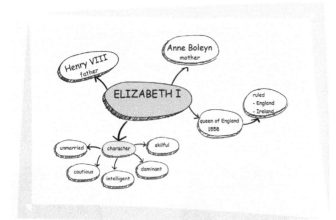

The research shows a clear winner for revision methods - **self-testing**. A good way to do this is with **flash cards**. Flash cards are really useful for helping you recall short – but important – pieces of information, like names and dates.

Side A - question

Side B - answer

Write questions on one side of the cards, and the answers on the back. This makes answering the questions and then testing yourself easy. Put all the cards you get right in a pile to one side, and only repeat the test with the ones you got wrong - this will force you to work on your weaker areas.

pile with right answers

pile with wrong answers

As this book has a quiz question structure itself, you can use it for this technique.

Another good revision method is **self-explanation**. This is where you explain how and why one piece of information from your course linked with another piece.

This can be done with **mind-maps**, where you draw the links and then write explanations for how they connect. For example, President Truman is connected with anti-communism because of the Truman Doctrine.

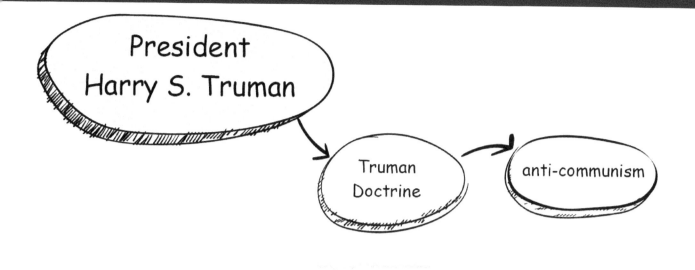

Review

Self-Test

Apply

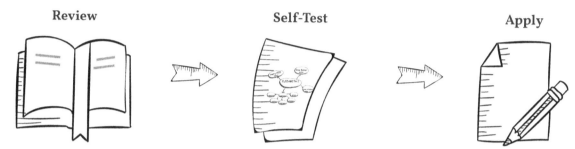

Start by highlighting or re-reading to create your flashcards for self-testing.

Test yourself with flash cards. Make mind maps to explain the concepts.

Apply your knowledge on practice exam questions.

Which revision techniques should I be cautious about?

Highlighting and **re-reading** are not necessarily bad strategies - but the research does say they're less effective than flash cards and mind-maps.

Highlighting

Re-reading

If you do use these methods, make sure they are **the first step to creating flash cards.** Really engage with the material as you go, rather than switching to autopilot.

DICTATORSHIP AND CONFLICT IN THE USSR, 1924 TO 1953

TIMELINE

1924 — *January 1924* - Lenin died *(p.63)*

1925 — Defeat of Trotsky in the leadership struggle *(p.17)*

1927 — Defeat of the United Opposition in the leadership struggle *(p.17)*

1928 — Defeat of the Right Opposition in the leadership struggle *(p.17)*

June 1928 - First Five Year Plan *(p.24)*

1928 - Collectivisation began *(p.27)*

1929 — De-Kulakisation began

1932 — The Great Famine began *(p.29)*

1933 — *January 1933* - Second Five Year Plan *(p.25)*

1934 — *December 1934* - Murder of Kirov started the Purges *(p.62)*

1936 — *June 1936* - The Family Code was introduced *(p.45)*

July 1936 - The Great Purge began and the first show trial *(p.31)*

December 1936 - 1936 Constitution introduced *(p.40)*

1937 — *January 1937* - The Trial of 17 *(p.32)*

1938 — *March 1938* - The Trial of 21 - the last show trial *(p.32)*

January 1938 - Third Five Year Plan *(p.26)*

1940 — *June 1940* - Labour Code introduced *(p.43)*

August 1940 - Trotsky was assassinated in Mexico *(p.67)*

1941 — *June 1941* - Nazi Germany invaded the USSR in Operation Barbarossa *(p.53)*

1942 — *August 1942* - Battle of Stalingrad began *(p.56)*

1945 — *April 1945* - The Red Army attacked Berlin *(p.57)*

May 1945 - Germany surrendered *(p.57)*

1946 — Fourth Five Year Plan *(p.59)*

1949 — Leningrad Affair *(p.34)*

1953

January 1953 - Doctor's Plot *(p.34)*

March 1953 - Death of Stalin *(p.66)*

CONTENDERS IN THE LEADERSHIP STRUGGLE, 1924-1929

There was no clear successor when Lenin died.

? What were the strengths of the contenders in the leadership struggle in Russia?

The contenders in the struggle for the leadership of Russia all had their own unique strengths and weaknesses. Any of them could have succeeded Lenin.

What were the strengths of Stalin as a contender in the leadership struggle in Russia?

Stalin *(p.64)* had 6 main strengths:

☑ He was the general secretary of the party in 1922, which gave him a lot of power as he could control what was discussed in the Politburo meetings.

☑ He could appoint his supporters to key jobs because he was general secretary.

☑ He had access to 26,000 personal files which he could use against the other contenders.

☑ He launched the Lenin Enrolment programme from 1923 to 1925. This recruited over 500,000 largely uneducated and poor members who were loyal to him.

☑ Many members favoured his idea of socialism in one country, where they would concentrate on developing communism in the USSR rather than worldwide.

☑ Most of the leading communists underestimated Stalin *(p.64)* and viewed him as merely a capable administrator.

What were the weaknesses of Stalin as a contender in the leadership struggle in Russia?

Stalin *(p.64)* had 4 main weaknesses:

☑ Stalin *(p.64)* was harshly criticised by Lenin in his 'Testament'. If this became public knowledge it would undermine him.

☑ He had angered Lenin by being very rude to Lenin's wife, Krupskaya.

☑ He did not take part in the October Revolution.

☑ He was not popular or well-known in the party, considering his relatively high level of responsibility within it. He had been famously described as 'the grey blur' - a bureaucrat and administrator, rather than a charismatic leader.

What were Trotsky's strengths as a contender in the leadership struggle in Russia?

Trotsky had 4 main strengths:

☑ He played a significant role in the October Revolution, working closely with Lenin.

☑ He enabled the communists to win the civil war by creating the Red Army.

☑ He was a great speaker and organiser.

☑ He was popular with the younger and more radical members.

What were Trotsky's weaknesses as a contender in the leadership struggle in Russia?

Trotsky had 3 key weaknesses:

☑ He joined the Communist Party in 1917, so he was not seen as one of the 'Old Bolsheviks'.

☑ He was disliked by members of the party because he was Jewish and seen as arrogant and rude.

☑ Many members did not like his idea of worldwide revolution because it meant a continued struggle and possible war.

What were Kamenev's strengths as a contender in the leadership struggle in Russia?

Kamenev 2 main strengths were:

☑ He had joined the party in 1903, so he was seen as an 'Old Bolshevik'.

☑ He was the party secretary in Moscow, which gave him a power base.

Quizzes, amazing exam preparation tools and more at GCSEHistory.com

What were Kamenev's weaknesses as a contender in the leadership struggle in Russia?

Kamenev's 2 key weaknesses were:

- ☑ He was seen as disloyal to Lenin because he had opposed Lenin's plans for the timing of the October Revolution.
- ☑ He was not really involved in the civil war.

What were Zinoviev's strengths as a leadership contender in Russia?

Zinoviev's 3 main strengths were:

- ☑ He had a strong party base because he was the party secretary in Leningrad.
- ☑ He was considered an 'Old Bolshevik' because he joined the party in 1903.
- ☑ He was a close friend of Lenin.

What were Zinoviev's weaknesses as a contender in the leadership contender in Russia?

Zinoviev's 3 key weaknesses were:

- ☑ He was seen as disloyal to Lenin because he had opposed Lenin's plans for the timing of the October Revolution.
- ☑ He was not heavily involved in the civil war.
- ☑ He was seen as ineffectual.

What were Bukharin's strengths as a contender for leadership in Russia?

Bukharin's 4 main strengths were:

- ☑ Lenin described him as the 'golden boy' of the Communist Party - he was very popular.
- ☑ He supported Lenin until his death.
- ☑ He played an important role in the Communist Party between 1925 and 1928.
- ☑ He was the editor of the communist newspaper, Pravda.

What were Bukharin's weaknesses as a contender in the leadership struggle in Russia?

Bukharin's 3 main weaknesses were:

- ☑ He had disagreed with Lenin over the ending of the First World War and the signing of the Treaty of Brest-Litovsk.
- ☑ He supported the New Economic Policy, which made him unpopular with the party's left wing.
- ☑ He was seen as too young and inexperienced.

DID YOU KNOW?

Stalin went on to remove Trotsky from photos where he stood with Lenin to give the impression the two had never been close.

HOW STALIN WON THE LEADERSHIP STRUGGLE, 1924-1929

Stalin outmanoeuvred his political opponents in the leadership struggle.

What was the leadership struggle in Russia?

After the death of Lenin in 1924, Stalin *(p.64)* ultimately won the leadership contest to rule Russia. He used different methods to do this, including using the power he had from his position as general secretary, playing his rivals off against each other, and using a pragmatic approach to win.

When did Stalin defeat his rivals in the leadership struggle in Russia?

Stalin *(p.64)* defeated his rivals in the leadership struggle between 1924 and 1929.

Who were Stalin's rivals in leadership struggle in Russia?

Stalin's *(p.64)* rivals in the leadership struggle after Lenin's death were: Trotsky, Kamenev, Zinoviev and Bukharin.

Why was there a leadership struggle in Russia after Lenin's death?

There was no clear successor to Lenin after he died. Lenin had not left instructions as to who should be the new leader of the Communist Party, nor who would lead the USSR. Therefore, there was a power struggle between 5 different candidates.

What did Lenin say about the individuals involved in the Russian leadership struggle?

Lenin wrote his 'Testament' in December 1922, after his second stroke, as he realised he was likely to die soon. In it, he criticised all of the men who might replace him. Lenin said:

- ☑ Trotsky was the most capable, but far too arrogant.
- ☑ Stalin *(p.64)* was too powerful, too rude, and he should be dismissed as party secretary.
- ☑ Kamenev had not supported Lenin's October Revolution, and so should not be trusted.
- ☑ Zinoviev had not supported Lenin's October Revolution, and so should not be trusted.
- ☑ Bukharin was the favourite of the party members, but Lenin felt he did not fully understand Marxism.

What did Stalin do first in the leadership struggle in the Soviet Union?

Stalin *(p.64)* immediately acted strategically in 4 main ways to secure the leadership of the Soviet Union:

- ☑ He organised Lenin's funeral and carried his coffin to present himself as a close friend and loyal supporter.
- ☑ Trotsky did not attend the funeral. He claimed Stalin *(p.64)* deliberately told him the incorrect date so it would appear as if he didn't respect Lenin.
- ☑ In May 1924, Kamenev, Zinoviev and Stalin *(p.64)* all agreed to not release Lenin's 'Testament', the document dictated by Lenin in December 1922.
- ☑ This meant fewer people knew about Lenin's criticisms of the members of the Communist Party who were candidates to become the new leader. This included the harsh criticisms of Stalin *(p.64)*.

What was the split in the Communist Party that Stalin exploited in the leadership struggle in Russia

The Communist Party was split between the left wing and the right wing:

- ☑ The right wing wanted to continue the New Economic Policy to slowly industrialise and favoured the idea of socialism in one country, ie building communism in the USSR.
- ☑ The left wing wanted to abandon the NEP, and have rapid industrialisation and worldwide revolution.

How did Stalin eliminate his rivals in the leadership struggle in Russia?

Stalin *(p.64)* was very clever. He divided and conquered his rivals in 3 stages:

- ☑ Stage 1: Stalin *(p.64)* united with Zinoviev and Kamenev to attack and isolate Trotsky.
- ☑ Stage 2: Stalin *(p.64)* united with Bukharin to attack the United Opposition of Zinoviev, Kamenev and Trotsky.
- ☑ Stage 3: Stalin *(p.64)* turned on Bukharin to attack the Right Opposition.

 ### How did Stalin eliminate his rivals in the leadership struggle in Stage 1 in Russia?

Stalin *(p.64)* took 3 key actions in Stage 1:

- ☑ In 1924, Stalin *(p.64)* allied with Zinoviev and Kamenev to remove Trotsky. They supported the New Economic Policy against Trotsky, who supported rapid industrialisation.
- ☑ Zinoviev and Kamenev undermined Trotsky and worked against him at the Thirteenth Party Congress in 1924 so that all of his ideas were rejected.
- ☑ As a result, Trotsky lost his job as Commissar for War in 1925.

 ### How did Stalin eliminate his rivals in the leadership struggle in Stage 2 in Russia?

Stalin *(p.64)* took 4 key actions in Stage 2:

- ☑ In 1927, Stalin *(p.64)* allied with Bukharin and supported the NEP against the United Opposition of Zinoviev, Kamenev and Trotsky.
- ☑ The United Opposition hoped to gain support for their ideas of rapid industrialisation and world revolution at the Fifteenth Party Congress in 1927.
- ☑ Stalin *(p.64)* accused Trotsky, Zinoviev and Kamenev of 'factionalism' which Lenin had banned in 1921. This was because they had formed a group which was against the party's New Economic Policy.
- ☑ Therefore, Trotsky, Zinoviev and Kamenev were expelled from the party in 1927. Trotsky withdrew from Soviet politics and went into exile.

 ### How did Stalin eliminate his rivals in the leadership struggle in Stage 3 in Russia?

Stalin *(p.64)* took 3 key actions in Stage 3:

- ☑ In 1928, he switched his support to rapid industrialisation, attacking Bukharin and the Right Opposition.
- ☑ Bukharin disagreed with Stalin *(p.64)* over abandoning the New Economic Policy, and began plotting with Kamenev to stop him.
- ☑ Bukharin's plotting was discovered and he was expelled from the Politburo in 1929.

Why was Stalin able to win the leadership struggle in 1929 in Russia?

There were 7 important reasons why Stalin *(p.64)* won the power struggle in 1929:

- ☑ His rivals made mistakes.
- ☑ Stalin *(p.64)* was able to exploit the division in the party over policy choices. Stalin switched his allegiance from the NEP to rapid industrialisation to attack his rivals.
- ☑ Being the general secretary meant Stalin *(p.64)* could put his supporters into positions that mattered, such as the Party Congress, to vote against his rivals.
- ☑ Stalin *(p.64)* was a very clever politician. He used his position as general secretary to undermine his rivals and he switched alliances to benefit his own position.
- ☑ He used his position as general secretary to pack the Thirteenth Party Congress in 1924 and the Fifteenth Party Congress in 1927 with his supporters.
- ☑ He took a pragmatic approach to policy. He supported Lenin's New Economic Policy between 1924 and 1928, when it appeared to be working, so he could attack the Left Opposition, but he switched to supporting rapid industrialisation in 1928 when NEP was becoming unpopular.
- ☑ He was lucky. For example, in 1923 when Lenin was dying, Trotsky also fell ill and was unable to compete with Stalin *(p.64)*.

What mistakes did Stalin's rivals make in the leadership struggle in Russia?

Stalin's *(p.64)* rivals made 2 key mistakes:

- ☑ Zinoviev and Kamenev had trusted Stalin *(p.64)* and worked with him to keep Trotsky out of power.
- ☑ Zinoviev and Kamenev agreed to not publish Lenin's 'Testament', which had severely criticised Stalin *(p.64)*.

 What was the title of the leader of the USSR after the leadership struggle in Russia?

When Stalin *(p.64)* had eliminated his rivals and took control of the country, he kept his existing title, General Secretary of the Communist Party of the Soviet Union.

DID YOU KNOW?

Stalin was born Josef Vissarionovich Djugashvili.
He changed his name to Stalin, which came from the Russian for 'man of steel'.

NEW ECONOMIC POLICY, 1921-1928

The New Economic Policy was a retreat from the government having complete control of the economy.

? **What was the NEP?**

The New Economic Policy (NEP) was the Soviet government's economic policy. It represented a temporary retreat from its previous policy of War Communism.

⧗ **When was the NEP introduced?**

The New Economic Policy was introduced in 1921 and lasted until 1928.

Why was the NEP introduced?

There were 4 key reasons why the NEP was introduced:

- ☑ The previous economic policy of War Communism had resulted in economic collapse and famine in some areas of the USSR.
- ☑ War Communism had also resulted in massive unrest among the workers and the number of strikes increased.
- ☑ The peasants had risen up in protest against War Communism with one of the most serious revolts in Tambov, requiring 50,000 Red Army soldiers to crush it.
- ☑ The Kronstadt Mutiny in March 1921, by the sailors in the Kronstadt Naval base made the Bolsheviks realise the dangers of continuing with the policy of War Communism.

How did the NEP work?

The NEP worked with 5 key features:

- ☑ Private ownership of businesses or banks that employed less than 20 people was allowed.
- ☑ Grain requisitioning from the peasants was stopped. Instead, they could sell it, keep the money and pay tax on anything they sold at a rate of 10%.
- ☑ The government kept control of heavy industry (coal, electricity, metal etc) and any large businesses.
- ☑ Money was reintroduced and so were some other aspects of the free market.

✅ People now had to pay taxes, first in goods and later in cash.

Who were the opponents of the NEP?

Some communists were disappointed with the NEP. They opposed it because they felt it betrayed their communist principles. Trotsky was one of those who opposed the NEP.

What were the positive effects of the NEP?

There were 5 key positive effects of the NEP:

✅ Grain production had increased by 50% by 1923.

✅ In 1922 the government introduced a new currency, called chervonets, which helped to stabilise the value of money.

✅ The prices of factory-made goods increased and there was greater demand for manufactured goods, especially from the countryside.

✅ There were fewer strikes and less discontent in the countryside.

✅ Trade with foreign countries increased, which helped the USSR financially.

What were the negative effects of the NEP?

There were 7 main negative effects of the NEP:

✅ Trade with other countries remained lower than that of 1913.

✅ Inequality also increased as some private business owners became richer. These were called NEPmen.

✅ Grain production increased, but it still wasn't enough to export large enough quantities abroad to get enough hard currency to fund industrialisation.

✅ Agriculture was still incredibly backwards.

✅ In 1923, there was the 'Scissors Crisis'. This was when food prices fell due to the supply of food increasing. However, the price of manufactured goods increased due to a shortage of manufactured goods. This made it difficult for peasants, who were earning less, and struggling to buy manufactured goods.

✅ Due to the Scissors Crisis the government forced the peasants to cut food prices. The peasants responded by feeding grain to their animals as meat was more expensive, meaning they made more money. By 1927, the amount of grain the government received decreased.

✅ Politically, Lenin came up against a lot of criticism as he was seen to have moved away from communist principles.

How did the NEP affect women?

In general, women's economic position worsened in 3 key ways as a result of the NEP.

✅ They were forced to give up their jobs for demobilised soldiers.

✅ The government did not see women's rights as a priority, and investment in the service industries was reduced.

✅ Following the revolution, gender equality only improved slightly.

Why was there opposition to the NEP?

There were 4 main reasons why different groups opposed the NEP:

✅ Some Bolsheviks saw the NEP as a return to capitalism because it allowed people and small, privately owned businesses to make a profit. This was not acceptable to them and they believed the policy of War Communism was more aligned to their beliefs.

✅ The workers still suffered because of the increase in food prices, while unemployment increased and real wages only passed the 1914 level by 1928. In reality, workers were struggling to afford basic necessities.

✅ Some peasants were getting richer and there was growing inequality between the richer peasants called 'Kulaks' and ordinary peasants.

✅ Women were hit particularly hard as many were forced out of their jobs when the Red Army demobilised after the civil war and they ended up on the streets.

INDUSTRIALISATION

The aim of industrialisation was to transform the USSR into a modern nation.

What was industrialisation?

Industrialisation was the process of accelerating the development of the Soviet Union to transform it from a backward country into a modern economy that could compete with the capitalist West.

When did Stalin focus on industrialisation in the Soviet Union?

Stalin *(p.64)* focused on rapid industrialisation of the USSR happened between May 1929 and June 1941.

Why did industrialisation happen in the USSR?

There were 6 main reasons why Stalin *(p.64)* wanted to industrialise the USSR:

- ☑ To prove himself to be the true successor of Lenin by continuing his work, and therefore, improving his own reputation as leader.
- ☑ By 1927, Stalin *(p.64)* feared the capitalist West would invade the USSR. The USSR needed to be able to modernise its army and mass produce weapons.
- ☑ According to Marxist theory, an advanced industrialised society was required for communism to flourish.
- ☑ The New Economic Policy seemed to have stalled as there was increasing unemployment, and in some areas of the economy the USSR had not yet reached the production levels of 1913.
- ☑ Politically, by changing his support from the NEP to rapid industrialisation, Stalin *(p.64)* was able to eliminate his opponents on the right of the Communist Party, such as Bukharin, in the leadership struggle.
- ☑ By introducing the Five Year Plans, he would increase his power and control over the USSR, as it would mean Moscow would have economic control over the whole of the country.

How did the Soviet Union go through the process of industrialisation?

The USSR developed a command economy in which industrialisation was organised through central planning under the Five Year Plans. These 4 main steps were followed:

- ☑ The Communist Party set targets for production for the whole of the USSR.
- ☑ The Gosplan *(p.23)*, or the State Committee for Planning, transformed these overall targets to create targets for each different industry, such as coal or electricity, for each region of the country.
- ☑ Each region would then set targets for each factory, mine or workshop.
- ☑ Each factory would set targets for each foreman, who in turn set targets for individual workers.

What were the successes of Soviet industrialisation?

Industrialisation under the Five Year Plans had 6 main successes:

- ☑ The USSR became more industrialised and was far more advanced in 1941 than it was in 1929, especially in heavy industry (coal, steel, iron, electricity).

- [x] Transport improved with an increase in railways and canals.
- [x] Industrial production levels increased dramatically from 1928 to 1939. For example, coal production increased from 35.5 million tons to 165.9 in 1940 - almost a fivefold increase.
- [x] The USSR was able to fight Nazi Germany in the Second World War because industrialisation had created a modern weapons industry.
- [x] The Five Year Plans helped create a larger working class as more industrial workers were needed in the cities and towns which led to people migrating from the countryside to the towns and cities. This would help develop a communist society.
- [x] Despite the country being ruined in the struggle against the Nazis during the Second World War, the USSR still managed to beat the USA to almost all of the major milestones in the Space Race.

 ## What were the failures of Soviet industrialisation?

There were 8 key failures of the industrialisation and the Five Year Plans:

- [x] The focus on heavy industry meant there were shortages in basic consumer goods, such as clothes and toiletries.
- [x] Working conditions were often appalling and dangerous.
- [x] Living conditions were awful and there was a shortage of housing.
- [x] The goods produced were often of poor quality as targets were based on quantity.
- [x] There was a lot of waste as the transport system wasn't efficient.
- [x] Targets were not met and were often unrealistic. This led to unreasonable pressure on the factories; workers and managers could be jailed for failing to meet targets.
- [x] It led to corruption, bribery and falsification of production figures.
- [x] The system was not flexible. It could not react to changes in circumstances because everything was planned in advance.

 ## What was the outcome of industrialisation in USSR?

There were 4 main results of industrialisation.

- [x] Heavy industry grew rapidly, and many industrial cities, such as Magnitogorsk, were built.
- [x] Unemployment almost vanished.
- [x] The USSR was able to re-arm and ultimately defeat Hitler in the Second World War.
- [x] There were shortages of consumer goods.

How did people benefit from Soviet industrialisation?

Industrialisation had 4 key benefits for ordinary people:

- [x] Women had greater job opportunities. In 1927, only 28% of industrial workers were female. This increased to 40% by 1940.
- [x] By the late 1930s, Soviet workers could get fairly well paid jobs and earn bonuses if they worked hard to meet their targets.
- [x] Unemployment was incredibly low.
- [x] Education was free and vocational education had been extended.

How were people negatively impacted by Soviet industrialisation?

Industrialisation had 6 key negative consequences for ordinary people:

- [x] Stalin's *(p.64)* priority was the industrialisation of the USSR. Therefore, the suffering of the ordinary people was of no consequence to him and was never dealt with.
- [x] Internal passports were introduced to prevent workers from finding, and moving to, better jobs as this would disrupt production.

- ☑ Factory discipline and punishments were harsh. Workers faced fines, the threat of dismissal, or even arrest for not meeting targets.
- ☑ Housing was never a priority for Stalin *(p.64)*. As a result, overcrowding with poor facilities was a huge issue.
- ☑ Stalin's *(p.64)* focus on heavy industry in his Five Year Plans meant there was a constant shortage of consumer goods.
- ☑ Many of the workers on the massive engineering projects were gulag *(p.35)* prisoners; thousands died because of the terrible working conditions.

DID YOU KNOW?

Industrialisation was successful in many ways - the USSR became a nuclear superpower.

However, the human cost of this was enormous.

FIVE YEAR PLANS

The Five Year Plans were the blueprints of how the USSR would be transformed.

What were the Five Year Plans?

The Five Year Plans were detailed economic plans drawn up to direct economic development. Each Five Year Plan was organised by Gosplan *(p.23)* and set targets for each industry by region, by factory and by individual workers. They were used to replace the New Economic Plan (NEP).

When were the Five Year Plans introduced?

The first Five Year Plan was started in 1928. Its focus was on developing heavy industry and collectivising agriculture.

Why replace the NEP with the Five Year Plan?

There were 4 main reasons why the NEP was replaced by the Five Year Plans:

- ☑ Stalin *(p.64)* wanted to rapidly industrialise as he feared attack from the capitalist West.
- ☑ Economically, the NEP had created a few issues such as high unemployment and it had only brought production back to 1913 levels.
- ☑ Ideologically, the NEP was seen as too capitalist as it allowed small privately owned businesses to exist which created more successful peasants (Kulaks), traders and retailers called NEP men. The Five Year Plans would end this.
- ☑ Politically, it helped Stalin *(p.64)* to remove his rival Bukharin during the leadership struggle because it isolated the right of Communist Party as it supported the NEP.

What were the successes of the Five Year Plans?

The greatest success of the Five Year Plans was that the USSR was industrialised and heavy industries such as coal, electricity and steel grew rapidly.

What were the failures of the Five Year Plans?

There were 3 key failures:

- ☑ Consumer goods were always neglected.
- ☑ Working and living conditions were awful.
- ☑ The targets that were set were never realistic and often not met.

What was the impact of the Five Year Plans on agriculture and the economy?

In farming, collectivisation was supposed to improve agricultural output. In reality, it led to starvation for millions in the Soviet Union. It was introduced so that excess grain could be sold abroad, with the profits used for industrialisation which was rapidly achieved.

What were the political aims of the Five Year Plans?

Stalin *(p.64)* wanted the USSR to rapidly industrialise as he feared attack from the capitalist West and he wanted to control the rural areas. Ideologically, he was opposed to the idea of capitalism which he believed the NEP supported. Stalin believed in Marxist principles.

What were the Marxist principles Stalin applied to the Five Year Plan?

Stalin *(p.64)* applied 5 Marxist principles to the Five Year Plan.

- ☑ Karl Marx believed that in a developed human society, countries would be industrialised.
- ☑ Factories should be made efficient and productive.
- ☑ There would be a steady move towards urbanisation.
- ☑ Fewer people would be needed to farm.
- ☑ Private property would be abolished and wealth would be redistributed to the poor.

What happened to the Five Year Plan after the war?

Stalin *(p.64)* announced the Fourth Five Year Plan after the Second World War:

- ☑ Its aim was to concentrate on rebuilding the USSR after the Second World War and focused on heavy industry and technology. An example of this was by 1950 Ukraine's industrial output surpassing that of its pre-war levels.
- ☑ Again, consumer goods were not prioritised and failed to meet the targets set.

> **DID YOU KNOW?**
>
> Other communist countries, such as the People's Republic of China, have used a similar method of planning the economy.

GOSPLAN

The Gosplan was responsible for creating the Five Year Plans.

What was the Gosplan?

Gosplan was the name for the 'State Committee for Planning', which was responsible for delivering the five year plans. Gosplan set targets for factory managers and workers and ensured they were achieved.

What was achieved by the Gosplan?

5,000 new factories were created between 1928 and 1937 under the planning and supervision of the Gosplan.

FIRST FIVE YEAR PLAN, 1928-32

The First Five Year Plan focused on developing the USSR into a modern, industrialised nation.

What was the Soviet Union's First Five Year Plan?

The First Five Year Plan was the first industrial plan created by Gosplan *(p. 23)* for the USSR.

When was the First Five Year Plan in the Soviet Union?

The First Five Year Plan was from October 1928 to December 1932.

What were the aims of the First 5 Year Plan in the Soviet Union?

The First Five Year Plan was focused on developing heavy industry such as steel, coal, iron and electricity. Approximately 80% of all investment went into heavy industry.

What were the successes of the First Five Year Plan in the Soviet Union?

The First Five Year Plan had 5 key successes:

- ☑ Electricity production trebled.
- ☑ The economy grew by 14% per year.
- ☑ Coal and iron output doubled and steel production increased by one-third.
- ☑ New industrial complexes were being built as well as machine tractor works.
- ☑ The targets were met in just four years, not five.

What were the weaknesses of the First Five Year Plan in the Soviet Union?

The First Five Year Plan had 5 key weaknesses:

- ☑ There was very little growth in consumer goods and fertilizers.
- ☑ The lack of skilled workers created instability, especially as many kept changing jobs.
- ☑ The quality of what was produced was low.
- ☑ Many targets were too high and not met, such as those in the chemical industry.
- ☑ Working and living conditions deteriorated further.

SECOND FIVE YEAR PLAN, 1933-37

The Second Five-Year Plan attempted to address some of the problems created by the first one.

? **What was the Soviet Union's Second Five Year Plan?**

The Second Five Year Plan was the second industrial plan created by Gosplan *(p.23)* for the USSR. It built on the work completed under the First Five Year Plan.

When was the Second Five Year Plan in the Soviet Union?

The Second Five Year Plan was from January 1933 to December 1937.

What were the aims of the Second Five Year Plan in the Soviet Union?

The 3 main aims of the Second Five Year Plan were:

☑ Still focused on developing heavy industry, but the targets were not so high.

☑ To develop communication.

☑ Higher targets for consumer goods to address the weaknesses of the First Five Year Plan.

What were the successes of the Second Five Year Plan in the Soviet Union?

The Second Five Year Plan had 5 main successes:

☑ By 1937, the USSR was self-sufficient in machine tool production and metal making.

☑ Transport and communications grew rapidly with the completion of such projects as the Moscow Metro.

☑ Chemical industries grew.

☑ Heavy industry benefitted from large scale projects being completed, such as Magnitogorsk Steel Plant and the Dnieper Dam.

☑ There were increases in heavy industry. For example, steel production increased four-fold.

What were the weaknesses of the Second Five Year Plan in the Soviet Union?

The Second Five Year Plan had 3 key weaknesses:

☑ There still was insufficient consumer goods and they failed to reach their targets.

☑ The Second Five Year Plan was disrupted due to the Great Purges.

☑ Oil production was poor.

DID YOU KNOW?

The White Sea Canal was one major project that happenes as a result of the Five Year Plans.

However, many workers died during its construction and it was not a major success as it was too narrow and too shallow in some places for the larger ships it was supposed to carry.

THIRD FIVE YEAR PLAN, 1938-41

The Third Five Year Plan was brought to an end by the Second World War.

What was the Soviet Union's Third Five Year Plan?

The Third Five Year Plan was the third industrial plan created by Gosplan *(p.23)* for the USSR. It built on the work completed under the Second Five Year Plan.

When was the Third Five Year Plan in the Soviet Union?

The Third Five Year Plan was from January 1938 to December 1941.

What were the aims of the Third Five Year Plan in the Soviet Union?

The Third Five Year Plan was still focused on developing heavy industry as there was a need for armaments to prepare for the Second World War.

What were the successes of the Third Five Year Plan in the Soviet Union?

The Third Five Year Plan had 2 main successes:

- ☑ Heavy industry grew.
- ☑ Defence and armaments grew quickly as one-third of investment was spent on them. This was the basis of a very strong armaments industry which was used during the Cold War.

What were the weaknesses of the Third Five Year Plan in the Soviet Union?

The Third Five Year Plan had 5 main weaknesses:

- ☑ The growth in steel output was poor.
- ☑ The plan was impacted by the Nazi Germany's invasion of the Soviet Union and it was ended early.
- ☑ The purges continued to impact the delivery of targets.
- ☑ Consumer good production suffered as resources had been diverted to the armaments industry.
- ☑ Oil production failed to meet its target and there was a fuel shortage.

DID YOU KNOW?

Stalin said: 'We are fifty or a hundred years behind the advanced countries. We must make up this gap in ten years. Either we do it or they will crush us.'

THE STAKHANOVITE MOVEMENT

The Stakhanovite movement provided inspiration to workers to work harder.

What was the Stakhanovite movement?

The Stakhanovite movement was the name given to workers that attempted to produce more than their targets, often by experimenting with new production techniques.

Who started the Stakhanovite movement?

Aleksei Stakhanov started the movement.

Quizzes, amazing exam preparation tools and more at GCSEHistory.com

Why did Alexei Stakhanov start the Stakhanovite movement?

He was a coal miner who was extremely competitive and focused on ways to improve productivity.

What did Alexei Stakhanov do in the Stakhanovite movement?

Stakhanov did the following 4 main things:

- ☑ He and his team managed to mine 102 tons of coal in less than six hours - 14 times more than his quota on 30th August, 1935!
- ☑ He received a holiday, a new home and extra pay as a reward.
- ☑ He was held up by the Soviet Union as an example to other workers and became a national hero.
- ☑ He travelled the country as a celebrity and appeared on the cover of 'Time' magazine.

What were the results of the Stakhanovite movement?

There were 3 main results of the movement:

- ☑ It sometimes disrupted the otherwise smooth running of factories as Stakhanovites attempted to set new records for production.
- ☑ The Stakhanovite movement was used as propaganda.
- ☑ It encouraged workers to work harder as they were promised higher wages or more rations.

DID YOU KNOW?

George Orwell's famous allegorical novel, 'Animal Farm', represents the Stakhanovite movement through the character of a horse called Boxer.

The horse's motto is: 'I will work harder!'

COLLECTIVISATION, 1930S

Collectivisation fulfilled economic and political goals for Stalin.

What was collectivisation in the USSR?

Collectivisation was a policy of uniting small individual farms into larger collective farms. There were different types of collective farms. 'Kolkhozes' were farms where the peasants 'owned' the land, while 'Sovkhoz' were state-owned farms. This was enforced by the Soviet government in the late 1920s - early 1930s.

When was collectivisation introduced in the USSR?

Collectivisation was announced in 1927, encouraged by the government in 1928 and then enforced in 1929.

What happened to the peasants under Soviet collectivisation?

Under collectivisation, peasants were forced to share resources and work to government targets. Any profits left after state demands were met were shared equally among members of the collectives.

Why did Stalin bring in collectivisation in the USSR?

There were 7 important reasons why Stalin *(p.64)* brought in collectivisation:

- ☑ Ideologically, it would socialise the peasants and turn them into good communists by getting rid of private farms and removing class divisions by destroying the kulaks.
- ☑ Economically, collectivisation would fund industrialisation by increasing food production to feed the workers and to sell grain abroad.
- ☑ Collectivisation would enable farming to be mechanised which would free workers for the industrialisation process.
- ☑ Politically, collectivisation would increase the Communists Party's control over the countryside.
- ☑ Politically, it would enhance Stalin's (p.64) reputation in a similar way as the introduction of the Five Year Plans had.
- ☑ Politically, it would help Stalin (p.64) remove Bukharin as a rival in the leadership struggle as he favoured the NEP.
- ☑ Between 1927 and 1928, the government struggled to get enough grain to feed the workers in the towns because of the 'Scissors Crisis'. The peasants hoped that by reducing grain production it would push up prices. Collectivisation would stop this from happening.

How was collectivisation brought into the USSR?

There were 4 key ways in which collectivisation took place:

- ☑ Propaganda, force and terror were all used.
- ☑ Initially, voluntary collectivisation was tried, but failed as the peasants resisted it and killed their animals as well as the officials sent to collectivise them.
- ☑ In December 1929, Stalin (p.64) announced the 'liquidation of the kulaks as a class', also known as dekulakisation, and any peasant that opposed collectivisation was labelled a 'kulak (p.30)' and attacked.
- ☑ Stalin (p.64) enlisted an army of 25,000 party activists called the Twenty-Five Thousanders to force the collectivisation of the farms and to identify kulaks.

What were the consequences during collectivisation in the USSR for peasants who refused to collectivise?

The following happened to peasants that refused to cooperate:

- ☑ They were branded a 'kulak' (p.30), and became targets for persecution.
- ☑ Around 30,000 kulaks were killed between 1930 and 1931.
- ☑ Up to 10 million were transported to labour camps in Siberia, where many were worked to death.

What were the initial problems with Soviet collectivisation?

Initially, there were 2 main problems with collectivisation:

- ☑ Both the richer and poorer peasants resented the government interfering in their lives.
- ☑ Peasants frequently destroyed their own crops and slaughtered their animals rather than hand them over to the communists.

What were the key features of Kolkhozes, or collective farms, during collectivisation in the USSR?

The 5 key features of a Kolkhoz were:

- ☑ All land, tools and livestock were shared.
- ☑ The government decided what was grown, the hours worked and what jobs were to be done. The peasants were controlled so they could not leave the Kolkhoz.
- ☑ They consisted of 50 to 100 households.
- ☑ The government took most of the produce and paid very low prices so the farmers were paid very little.
- ☑ Families could have an acre of land to grow vegetables or keep animals.

What was the role of machine tractor stations during collectivisation in the USSR?

Machine Tractor Stations, or MTS, were:

- ☑ Created so collective farms could rent machinery such as tractors.

- ☑ Created to control the peasants as they were run by the Communist Party.
- ☑ Used to oversee the collective farms to ensure compliance.
- ☑ Problematic. It was costly for the peasants to rent machinery as there wasn't enough of it and it was poorly maintained.

 What were the successes of Soviet collectivisation?

Collectivisation had 6 main successes:

- ☑ Farms were collectivised. In 1931, over 50% of households were collectivised. By the end of 1934, 70% of peasant households were in collectives. This increased to 90% by 1936.
- ☑ By the end of 1931, 22.8 million tonnes of grain had been collected. This was enough to feed the cities and export to fund industrialisation.
- ☑ It broke peasant resistance and destroyed the kulaks.
- ☑ It enabled rural areas to be turned communist.
- ☑ It meant the Communist Party extended its control over rural areas.
- ☑ There was enough machinery and changes in farming methods for peasants to be freed up so they could move to work in the new factories.

 What were the failures of collectivisation in the USSR?

There were 4 main failures of collectivisation:

- ☑ Peasant opposition severely reduced production levels which took years to recover. Grain production did not exceed pre-collectivisation levels until 1935. Meat production did not return to pre-collectivisation levels until 1955.
- ☑ The USSR's agricultural technology did not improve.
- ☑ The machine tractor stations failed to deliver what was needed in terms of enough working machinery.
- ☑ The policy contributed to the Great Famine of 1932 - 1933. In the spring of 1932, a famine began in Ukraine and other areas (north Caucasus, Kazakhstan). By late 1934, approximately 7 million people had died.

 How was collectivisation used to oppress Ukraine during collectivisation in the USSR?

Collectivisation was used to oppress Ukraine in 6 key ways:

- ☑ Ukraine, which was part of the Soviet Union, was a state with rich farmland.
- ☑ Lots of Ukrainians refused to join the collective farms. Those who resisted were brutally oppressed.
- ☑ Stalin *(p.64)* wanted to destroy Ukrainian nationalism and culture because of this opposition.
- ☑ The government increased the grain quotas, despite food production decreasing between 1932 and 1933.
- ☑ Officials took everything from the peasants when they could not meet the quotas.
- ☑ Thus, Ukraine suffered greatly during the Great Famine of 1932 - 1933, which is also called the 'Holodomor' - meaning 'death by hunger'.

 How did collectivisation in the USSR contribute to the Great Famine?

Collectivisation made the Great Famine of 1932 - 1933 worse in 4 key ways:

- ☑ It severely disrupted farming which resulted in a decrease in production.
- ☑ The peasants resisted it by killing their animals and destroying their crops which meant there would be less food produced in subsequent years.
- ☑ The new collective farms were often badly run by the Twenty-Five Thousanders, who had little farming experience. This was the name given to workers from industrial cities who voluntarily left their homes to work on the frontline in rural areas.
- ☑ Many of the most experienced farmers were either deported, imprisoned in the gulags or executed.

KULAKS

Kulaks were seen as enemies of the revolution.

Who were the kulaks?

Kulaks were peasants who were wealthy enough to own a farm and hire labour.

When were the kulaks attacked by the Communist government?

The kulaks were attacked by the Bolsheviks at 3 different times:

- ☑ Between 1918 and 1921, the Bolsheviks implemented their policy of War Communism. During this period, the kulaks were blamed for grain shortages as peasants resisted grain requisitioning.
- ☑ Between 1921 and 1928, the communists implemented their NEP. During this time, the kulaks were accused of being capitalists and against the revolution as they became richer.
- ☑ Between 1928 and 1932, the communists implemented collectivisation. The kulaks were accused of being capitalists and 'class enemies', and Stalin *(p.64)* launched a dekulakisation campaign.

Why were kulaks considered anti-communist?

The kulaks were considered anti-Communist due to 3 main reasons:

- ☑ They strongly opposed collectivisation as they wanted to own their farms.
- ☑ They didn't want to sell their grain to the government because purchasing prices were low.
- ☑ The Soviet government considered the kulaks to be capitalists and, therefore, enemies of communism.

What happened to the kulaks?

Kulaks were considered enemies of communism and most ended up in one of 3 categories during collectivisation:

- ☑ 'Counter-revolutionaries', who were to be shot or sent to the gulags.
- ☑ 'Active opponents of collectivisation', who were deported to other areas of the USSR.
- ☑ Those who were expelled from farms and forced to settle on poor land.

What was the impact of collectivisation on the kulaks?

Collectivisation destroyed the kulaks as a class and many were exiled, imprisoned in gulags, or executed.

THE PURGES, 1930-1953

Stalin's paranoia reached new heights in the Great Purge.

What were the purges?

The Soviet purges involved the mass arrests, imprisonment and executions of political prisoners, dissidents and people considered a threat to Stalin *(p.64)*.

When were the purges?

The Great Purge, also known as the Great Terror, took place between 1936 and 1938.

Who was in charge of carrying out the purges?

The purges were carried out by the secret police, or the People's Commissariat of Internal Affairs (NKVD *(p.34)*) under the leadership of:

- ☑ Yagoda from 1934 to 1936.
- ☑ Yezhov from 1936 to 1938.

Who was targeted by the purges?

A wide range of groups were targeted as 'enemies of the people':

- ☑ Members of the Communist Party, in particular Old Bolsheviks who had worked with Lenin, such as Kamenev and Zinoviev.
- ☑ Leading members in the Central Committee.
- ☑ The armed forces.
- ☑ Artists, writers and musicians.
- ☑ Kulaks.
- ☑ Priests.
- ☑ Scientists.

What were the reasons for the purges?

There were political and economic reasons for the purges.

What were the political reasons for the purges?

There were 8 political reasons for the purges:

- ☑ Stalin *(p.64)* was paranoid and he saw enemies and opposition everywhere.
- ☑ It would give Stalin *(p.64)* total control of the Communist Party and the country.
- ☑ People were incredibly unhappy because of the negative impact of collectivisation and industrialisation so there was more political opposition.
- ☑ There was growing political opposition in the Communist Party because of Stalin's *(p.64)* policies of rapid industrialisation and collectivisation.
- ☑ One leading Party member, Ryutin, openly criticised Stalin *(p.64)* in 1932. However, when Stalin demanded the death penalty, the Politburo, including Kirov, voted against it.
- ☑ At the 17th Party Congress in 1934, Kirov, a member of the Politburo, spoke out against rapid collectivisation and received a longer standing ovation than Stalin *(p.64)*.
- ☑ Kirov received more votes than Stalin *(p.64)* in the elections to the Central Committee so he had become a threat to Stalin's position as general secretary of the Party.
- ☑ On 1st December 1934, Sergei Kirov, was murdered and Stalin *(p.64)* claimed Kamenev, Zinoviev and Trotsky were to blame and used it as an excuse to start the purges.

What were the economic reasons for the purges?

There were 3 main economic reasons for the purges:

- ☑ Those targeted could be blamed for the economic issues, for example missed targets.
- ☑ Economically, the purges helped Stalin *(p. 64)* as they provided free labour from the gulags.
- ☑ The fear created by the purges could be used as a weapon to pressure people into meeting their economic targets.

What were the show trials during the purges?

Show trials were an important part of the purge:

- ☑ They were held for those with a high profile and people Stalin *(p. 64)* viewed as an enemy.
- ☑ The scripts were written beforehand and everyone already knew what the outcome would be.
- ☑ The accused were tortured into confessing, often to save their families.

When were the show trials during the purges?

The show trials occurred between 1936 and 1938.

Which were the most important show trials during the purges?

There three trials that were the most important:

- ☑ Trial of 16 in August 1936, which included Zinoviev and Kamenev.
- ☑ Trial of 17 in January 1937, of party officials.
- ☑ Trial of 21 in March 1938, which included Bukharin and Yagoda (ex-head of the NKVD *(p. 34)*).

What happened during the Trial of 16 during the purges?

The following 3 key events happened during the Trial of 16, in 1936:

- ☑ 16 people, including Zinoviev and Kamenev, were accused of disrupting the Five Year Plans and Kirov's murder.
- ☑ They were tortured and threatened so they would confess.
- ☑ They were executed.

What happened during the Trial of 17 during the purges?

The following 3 key events happened during the Trial of 17, in 1937:

- ☑ Party officials were accused of plotting to overthrow the government, disrupting the Five Year Plans and Kirov's murder.
- ☑ They were tortured and threatened so they would confess.
- ☑ Thirteen were executed and 4 sent to the Gulags.

What happened during the Trial of 21 during the purges?

The following 4 key events happened during the Trial of 21, in 1938:

- ☑ 21 people, including Bukharin and Yagoda (ex-head of the NKVD *(p. 34)*), were accused of plotting to overthrow the government, disrupting the Five Year Plans and Kirov's murder.
- ☑ They were tortured and threatened so they would confess.
- ☑ Bukharin attempted to speak out against show trials to prove that the trials were false and unjust.
- ☑ Again, the accused were executed.

What happened during the Great Purge?

There were 7 key events during the Great Purge:

- ☑ There were mass arrests, forced confessions and people were either executed or imprisoned in a Gulag *(p.35)*.
- ☑ The show trials of 1936 to 1938.
- ☑ The NKVD *(p.34)* relied on ordinary people to inform on their neighbours.
- ☑ Between 1936 and 1938, the terror escalated under the NKVD *(p.34)* leader, Yezhov. This period is called Yezhovshchina.
- ☑ From May 1937, the armed forces were purged starting with 8 generals, including Marshal Tukhachevsky, who was accused of plotting against Stalin *(p.64)*.
- ☑ In July 1937, Yezhov passed NKVD *(p.34)* Order 00447. This set quotas for how many people had to be arrested, of whom 28% were shot and the rest sent to Gulags.
- ☑ By the end of the purge of the military, all naval admirals and all but one air force commander had been executed, along with the majority of the army's command.

Why were many of the Old Bolsheviks executed during the purges?

Many 'Old Bolsheviks' who were part of the October 1917 revolution were killed during the purges because it enabled Stalin *(p.64)* to consolidate his position as the dictator of both the Communist Party and the USSR. Bukharin and Kamenev were among those he executed.

Why did the purges end?

There were 2 main reasons why Stalin *(p.64)* halted the purges by the end of 1938:

- ☑ They had destabilised society and were escalating out of control as neighbour turned on neighbour.
- ☑ They were disrupting the economy to such an extent that the targets of the Five Year Plans were not being met because key workers were caught up in the terror.

What were the results of the Great Purge?

The impact of the purges was significant in 4 main ways:

- ☑ The cost in human life was horrific, with an estimated 7 to 8 million arrested, 2 million dead in the gulags, and 1 to 1.5 million executed.
- ☑ Politically, Stalin *(p.64)* had created a personal dictatorship in which any opposition from within the party or outside had been killed off.
- ☑ Economically, the purges were a huge disruption as the experienced people needed to meet the targets of the Five Year Plans were removed from their jobs.
- ☑ Militarily, the purges meant that the USSR was less able to fight Nazi Germany when they invaded in 1941.

Were there purges during the Second World War?

There were 2 key purges during the Second World War:

- ☑ The Volga Germans were considered suspect when the Nazis invaded the USSR in 1941. Therefore, they were deported to Siberia.
- ☑ The USSR deported ethnic Finns and internally placed them in exile when Finland supported the Nazi invasion of the USSR *(p.53)*.

Who was targeted in purges after the Second World War?

There were 4 key groups that were purged after the Second World War:

- ☑ Nationalists.
- ☑ Soldiers who were German prisoners of war.
- ☑ The Leningrad Communist Party.
- ☑ Jews.

How were the Jews purged after the Second World War?

The Jews were purged after the Second World War in 3 key ways:

- ☑ Any Jewish person in a position of responsibility lost their job.
- ☑ Leaders of the Jewish community were arrested.
- ☑ In 1953, Stalin *(p.64)* claimed there was a 'Doctor's Plot' in which 10 Jewish doctors were plotting to assassinate him. It led to mass arrests but Stalin died before anything else happened.

What were the purges of soldiers after the Second World War?

After the Second World War, Soviet soldiers that had been German Prisoners of War were purged:

- ☑ 1.5 million Soviet soldiers that had been held as prisoners of war by Nazi Germany were returned to the USSR.
- ☑ They were considered traitors and deported to the Gulags in Siberia.

What were the purges of nationalists after the Second World War?

After the Second World War, nationalists were purged in 3 main ways:

- ☑ Some of the USSR's republics attempted to win their independence at the end of the war.
- ☑ Lithuania, Ukraine, Estonia and Latvia had all taken up arms against the USSR.
- ☑ In response, there were mass deportations.

How was the Communist Party purged after the Second World War?

After the Second World War, the Communist Party was purged:

- ☑ In 1949, Stalin *(p.64)* attacked the top party officials of the Leningrad Communist Party because he thought it was a threat.
- ☑ 200 members were arrested on charges of spying for Britain and corruption. Some members were shot, some were imprisoned and some were exiled.
- ☑ About 2,000 officials also lost their jobs.

DID YOU KNOW?

Nikolai Yezhov was the leader of the NKVD when the Great Purge escalated between 1936 and 1938.

He was nicknamed the 'Poisoned Dwarf' and some say he attended meetings with blood on his shirt after torturing his victims.

THE SECRET POLICE

The secret police had unimaginable power in the USSR.

Who were the secret police in the USSR?

The secret police was an organisation which had the job of eliminating any opposition to communist rule.

What were the secret police known as in the USSR?

The secret police were variously known as:

- ☑ The Cheka, or All-Russian Extraordinary Committee to Combat Counter-Revolution and Sabotage, from 1917 to 1922.
- ☑ The GPU, or State Political Directorate, in 1922.
- ☑ The OGPU, or All-Union State Political Board, from 1923.
- ☑ The NKVD, or People's Commissariat for Internal Affairs, from 1934 to 1953.
- ☑ KGB or ,Committee for State Security, from 1954.

What was the Soviet secret police's primary responsibility?

The secret police removed and suppressed all opposition:

- ☑ The Cheka committed the Red Terror during the Civil War.
- ☑ They participated in the attack on the kulaks during collectivisation.
- ☑ The NKVD carried out the Great Purge under Stalin *(p. 64)*.

What were the techniques of the Soviet Secret Police?

The secret police in the USSR used 4 main - and extreme - techniques:

- ☑ Mass arrests.
- ☑ Forced confessions under torture.
- ☑ Development of informant networks.
- ☑ Quotas were introduced in July 1937, with Order 00447 setting out how many arrests the NKVD was expected to make and how many people should be executed.

DID YOU KNOW?

The secret police operated outside the legal system in the USSR until after Stalin's death.

This meant it could act in ways considered illegal without being held accountable for its actions.

THE GULAGS

The gulags were a key tool of political repression and provided slave labour for the economy.

What were the gulags?

The Gulag was the government organisation established by Lenin to run forced labour camps. The camps themselves were also called gulags, after the name of the agency that set them up.

When were the gulags started?

The Gulag system was set up under Lenin in 1919.

What was the gulags' purpose?

There were 3 key reasons why the gulags were created:

- ☑ As a form of severe punishment.
- ☑ A way in which to get free labour from the inmates.
- ☑ As a deterrent to other people.

How did the Gulag system grow?

The Gulag system grew over time in 4 main stages:

- ☑ In 1919, the first gulags were opened under Lenin.
- ☑ In 1921, there were 84 camps.
- ☑ In 1929, there were approximately 179,000 prisoners.
- ☑ By 1950, there were approximately 2.5 million prisoners.

Who was put in the gulags?

The gulags were set up to accommodate 7 main groups of prisoners accused of a wide range of crimes:

- ☑ Political prisoners, such as those accused of plotting to overthrow the government and foreign communists accused of spying.
- ☑ Peasants, especially Kulaks, accused of sabotaging collectivisation.
- ☑ Workers and factory managers convicted of disrupting factory work and production.
- ☑ Leaders of different ethnic groups who wanted independence from the USSR.
- ☑ Ordinary criminals.
- ☑ Members of the armed forces.
- ☑ Any artists, writers or educators who were considered a threat.

Where were the gulags?

The gulags were particularly prevalent in the east of the Soviet Union, especially in Siberia.

How did the Soviet Union profit from the gulags?

The gulags provided a huge amount of slave labour, with prisoners forced to work in industry, on the massive industrial projects such as Moscow's metro and the White Sea Canal, and on the railways.

What were the conditions of the gulags?

Conditions in the gulags were terrible in 5 main ways:

- ☑ Food was rationed and tied to how much work prisoners completed.
- ☑ Rations were cut if prisoners did not meet their targets and so many prisoners died of starvation. Extra rations could be earned by working harder.
- ☑ The work was hard labour and tied to the targets of the Five Year Plans.
- ☑ Many prisoners died due to the work as it was so dangerous and difficult.
- ☑ The living conditions were awful; over crowded, with little sanitation and no heating. Many died of the cold.

DID YOU KNOW?

Gulag is an acronym for Glavnoe Upravlenie Lagerei.
This is Russian for 'Main Camp Administration'.

Quizzes, amazing exam preparation tools and more at GCSEHistory.com

STALIN'S CULT OF PERSONALITY

Stalin's cult of personality encouraged an almost God-like worship.

What was Stalin's cult of personality?

Stalin *(p.64)* wanted to be praised and adored. A 'cult of personality' was developed for him in the USSR to create adoration of him through the use or art and popular culture to improve his status as the leader and to inspire loyalty.

When did Stalin's cult of personality exist?

Stalin's *(p.64)* cult of personality developed in the 1920s and existed throughout his time as leader of the USSR.

Why was there a cult of Stalin?

There were 4 important reasons why Stalin *(p.64)* developed his cult of personality:

☑ To increase Stalin's *(p.64)* legitimacy and authority as Lenin's true successor.

☑ To unify the USSR around loyalty to one leader. This was a tradition in tsarist Russia where the tsar was seen as 'the little father'. Stalin's *(p.64)* cult of personality was an extension of this.

☑ It raised Stalin's *(p.64)* status above other members of the Party so he became all powerful.

☑ Rapid industrialisation and collectivisation had created great suffering in the USSR. The cult of personality could be used to direct dissatisfaction towards other leaders in the Communist Party, not Stalin *(p.64)*.

What was Stalin's image according to his cult of personality?

Stalin *(p.64)* had 4 main characteristics according to his cult.

☑ Stalin *(p.64)* was portrayed as a man of the people working alongside ordinary people. He was characterised as a 'father-figure', very much in the style of the tsars.

☑ He was portrayed as an economic expert and amazing economic planner. All forms of media sung the praises of Stalin *(p.64)* and his Five Year Plans.

☑ He was presented as a great thinker who understood communism and who was the true successor of Lenin. He was called 'Vozhd' which means leader.

☑ Stalin's *(p.64)* cult of personality developed after the Second World War. He became the 'Generalissimo' which portrayed him as the saviour of the USSR. Films depicted him as a hero; for example, he was shown defeating the Nazis in Berlin when he was never actually there.

How was Stalin's cult of personality created?

There were 4 key ways in which Stalin's *(p.64)* cult of personality was created:

☑ All images showed Stalin *(p.64)* in a positive way. Posters, paintings, photographs and films created a myth of Stalin as a hero.

☑ Stalin *(p.64)* was honoured in numerous ways. Towns, streets and buildings were named after him. There were statues of him in most towns and cities.

☑ History was rewritten to emphasise Stalin's *(p.64)* contribution to key events such as the October Revolution in 1917. Old photographs were altered to rewrite history.

☑ Stalin *(p.64)* was given many titles such as 'Brilliant Genius of Humanity'.

DID YOU KNOW?

The impact of his cult was so far-reaching that when Stalin died, in 1953, there was an outpouring of grief despite the fact he ruled over a country where millions were murdered in the Great Terror.

SOVIET PROPAGANDA UNDER STALIN

Soviet propaganda was a key feature of Stalin's government.

What was Soviet Union propaganda under Stalin?

Propaganda is information which tends to be deliberately biased or misleading, and it is used to promote a certain point of view. The Soviet government used propaganda to make its people believe certain things or have certain attitudes.

Why did the Soviet Union use propaganda?

Soviet propaganda had 2 key aims:

☑ To control the people of the Soviet Union.

☑ The Soviet government wanted to create the 'new Soviet man' and the 'new Soviet women' who would show desirable Socialist qualities e.g. care more about the community than the individual.

What methods of propaganda did the Soviet Union use?

There were 7 main methods of propaganda:

☑ Stalin's *(p.64)* cult of personality *(p.37)* used all forms of the media to create a specific image of Stalin as a heroic and all-knowing leader.

☑ All art and culture was controlled and the only official culture allowed was socialist realism *(p.39)*.

☑ Through different organisations such as the youth group, the Komsomol, or through education.

☑ By rewriting history and changing facts to suit the Soviet cause.

☑ All books, newspapers and magazines were controlled and written to support the Soviet government.

☑ Photographs were altered to suit the Soviet government's view of events.

☑ Radios were put up in public places such as work and clubs in the 1920s for group listening.

DID YOU KNOW?

The Communist Party used propaganda from the time of the revolutions through to the collapse of the USSR in 1991.

During the Civil War, Trotsky organised the Agitprop trains to spread the communist message across the country.

SOVIET CENSORSHIP UNDER STALIN

Soviet censorship was extensive; all information had to be controlled.

What was censorship under Stalin?

Censorship is the control of information in the media which could be considered unacceptable by the government. Under Stalin's *(p.64)* rule, the Soviet government had very strict control of information in terms of what people could see, hear or read.

Why did Stalin use censorship?

There were 3 main reasons why Stalin *(p.64)* used censorship:

☑ To control what people knew.

- ☑ To stop any criticism of him or the government.
- ☑ To stop any opposition developing or having the ability to undermine the government.

How did the communists implement censorship of the media?

There were 6 important ways to censor information:

- ☑ Lenin had banned all non-Bolshevik newspapers in 1917.
- ☑ The radio was also controlled by the Commission for Posts and Telegraph.
- ☑ Printing presses were nationalised by Lenin.
- ☑ The Communist Party had its own newspaper, Pravda (Truth).
- ☑ The Soviet government had its own newspaper called the Izvestiya (News).
- ☑ The government controlled what could be published using the Censorship Office or Glavlit which was controlled by the secret police.

How did censorship affect Soviet art and culture?

Censorship had a negative impact on art and culture as the quality of what was produced was reduced. Some artists refused to create any work.

What happened to people who broke the censorship laws in the Soviet Union?

Writers, journalists, artists or anyone who broke the censorship laws were punished in 2 main ways:

- ☑ They could be internally exiled which meant being sent to live in a different part of the USSR.
- ☑ They could be sent to a gulag. *(p.35)*

DID YOU KNOW?

Banned books were withdrawn from the public and put into special storage units.

Only members of the Communist Party with special clearance could access them.

SOCIALIST REALISM

Stalin favoured Socialist Realism.

What was the communist policy of socialist realism?

Socialist realism was a communist policy on art and culture which portrayed life under socialism in a positive way. It was focused on ordinary people.

When was the communist policy of socialist realism in force?

Socialist realism was official Communist Party policy from the 1930 to 1953 under Stalin's *(p.64)* rule.

Who was involved with the communist policy of socialist realism?

There were different people involved with the socialist realism movement:

- ☑ Stalin *(p.64)* ordered that all art and culture should follow the artistic style of socialist realism.
- ☑ The film director, Eisenstein, was very popular.

☑ In literature, writers Sholokhov, (1928's 'And Quiet Flows the Don'), and Kataev, (1932's 'Time Forward'), were popular.

How did the communist policy of socialist realism affect art?

Under socialist realism, art:

☑ Often showed peasants with plentiful harvests and successful industrial workers.

☑ Became part of Stalin's *(p.64)* cult of personality *(p.37)*.

☑ Showed happy and positive images of ordinary life in the Soviet Union.

How did the communist policy of socialist realism affect music and dance?

Under socialist realism, music and dance:

☑ Traditional folk music and dancing as well as ballet dancing were encouraged.

☑ Jazz music was banned.

How did the communist policy of socialist realism affect literature?

Under socialist realism, literature was:

☑ Focused on ordinary workers or peasants.

☑ Centred on life in the Soviet Union, such as a record-breaking shift in the steel factories or life on a collective farm. War and detective stories were also popular.

How did the communist policy of socialist realism affect cinema?

Under socialist realism, the cinema focused on glorious tales from Soviet or Russian history, such as the Russian Civil War.

DID YOU KNOW?

Stalin called writers and artists, 'engineers of the human soul'.

1936 CONSTITUTION

In reality the 1936 Soviet Constitution did not give the citizens any rights.

What was the Stalin Constitution?

The 1936 Soviet Constitution, also known as the Stalin *(p.64)* Constitution, redesigned the government of the Soviet Union.

When was the Stalin Constitution adopted?

The 1936 Soviet Constitution was adopted on 5th December, 1936.

Why was the constitution changed by Stalin?

The new constitution was introduced for 2 main reasons:

☑ To show the Soviet Union had changed since the 1924 constitution.

☑ In an attempt to improve the USSR's reputation with other countries.

What did the 1936 constitution include?

The 1936 Soviet Constitution include the following 5 main articles:

☑ It granted different rights and freedoms, such as the right to vote from the age of 18, to housing, and to care in old age and illness.

☑ It established direct elections of the government.

☑ It changed the name of the Central Executive Committee to the Supreme Soviet.

☑ Groups previously seen as enemies, such as the nobility and kulaks, would be seen as equal citizens.

☑ All of the 15 republics were renamed as Soviet Socialist Republics under Article 13. They were given the impression of a degree of autonomy but in reality they were controlled from Moscow.

 What impact did the 1936 constitution have?

The 1936 Constitution had little impact due to 3 main reasons:

☑ It was a piece of propaganda.

☑ The rights were not upheld as there were still mass arrests and the government used terror to control the population.

☑ Only Communist Party members could be elected to government.

DID YOU KNOW?

The 1936 Soviet Constitution listed many rights the people had.

However, it also confirmed the Communist Party as the only political party allowed, reaffirming the USSR as a one-party dictatorship.

LIVING IN TOWNS AND THE COUNTRYSIDE, 1924-41

Living conditions in the USSR were harsh as housing was not prioritised by the government.

 What were living conditions like in the Soviet Union?

Living conditions in the Soviet Union varied hugely. It depended on where you lived and who you were.

 What were the living conditions in the Soviet Union countryside like?

In the countryside the living conditions were poor in 4 main ways:

☑ There was only basic housing, with outside toilets and no running water.

☑ Peasants were not allowed to leave their farms and had passports for internal travel.

☑ There was rationing, which allowed Stalin *(p.64)* to confiscate excess food for distribution in the cities.

☑ The peasants received less food than the workers in the towns and cities and so had to travel to buy food.

 What were the living conditions like in the Soviet Union towns?

In the towns the living conditions were poor in 8 main ways:

☑ There was insufficient housing in towns and cities because industrialisation led to a rapid increase in the number of workers.

☑ Housing was of low quality and living standards were poor.

☑ Most lived communally, with several families sharing one apartment. Each family had one room for their whole family to live, but shared the kitchen and bathroom.

- ☑ Some people were 'corner dwellers' as they lived in a shed, a cupboard or, literally, the corner of a corridor.
- ☑ Food was not plentiful - queuing for food was a common occurrence in the Soviet Union during the 1930s. Food rationing was introduced between 1929 and 1935.
- ☑ There were shortages in everyday consumer goods such as toiletries and clothes.
- ☑ There were long queues for consumer goods when they were available.
- ☑ The Second World War made the situation worse as approximately 1/3 of urban housing was damaged or destroyed.

What did the government do to improve living conditions in towns in the Soviet Union?

The government tried to improve the towns and cities by providing leisure activities such as cinemas, parks and various sporting facilities.

What were the living conditions like in the new factory towns in the Soviet Union?

The living conditions in the new factory towns created by industrialisation were awful in 4 main ways:

- ☑ Many people lived in barracks or other forms of communal accommodation with not enough furniture.
- ☑ Sanitation was inadequate with insufficient washing facilities, running water or toilets. Disease thus spread quickly, leading to high sickness rates.
- ☑ There was little infrastructure such as proper roads, sewers or electricity.
- ☑ Living conditions were very slow to improve during the 1930s.

What were the living conditions of the party officials of the Soviet Union?

The living conditions for the party officials were very good in 2 main ways:

- ☑ Party officials lived in relative luxury, compared to ordinary people in the USSR. Their accommodation was larger and not communal.
- ☑ They had access to special shops where they could buy consumer goods as a reward for their loyalty, and access to more and better quality food.

DID YOU KNOW?

Housing was never prioritised by Stalin, even after the destruction caused by the Second World War.

It was only after Stalin's death in 1953 that massive housing projects were developed to meet demand.

WORKING IN TOWNS AND THE COUNTRYSIDE, 1924-41

Working conditions could be terrible in the USSR as health and safety was neglected.

What were working conditions like in the towns and countryside in the Soviet Union?

The working conditions in the towns and countryside in the Soviet Union were poor and often dangerous.

What were working conditions like in the towns in the Soviet Union?

Working conditions in the towns were difficult and it was very physically demanding in 5 main ways:

- ☑ Trade unions could not protect the workers from the poor working conditions or low pay because they had little power.

- ☑ Working conditions were dangerous. There were many accidents because health and safety was considered irrelevant.
- ☑ To encourage workers to work harder, piecework was introduced - people were paid by how much they produced. This meant working harder to increase wages.
- ☑ Workers did not have the right to leave their job to look for another one because of the internal passports.
- ☑ Stalin *(p.64)* brought in an incredibly harsh labour code in 1940, which set out harsh punishments for lateness with pay cuts, arrest for changing jobs without permission, and an increase in the hours and the number of days workers had to work.

What were working conditions like in the countryside in the Soviet Union?

The working conditions in the countryside on the collective farms were poor in 3 main ways:

- ☑ The pay was terrible and much lower than in the factories.
- ☑ It was very restrictive. They were told what to plant and when, and could not leave the collective farms without permission.
- ☑ The work was very physically demanding with long hours as there was a lack of machinery at the machine tractor stations.

What were the positives of the working conditions in the Soviet Union?

There were 4 main benefits to working:

- ☑ There was full employment, even if the jobs were terrible.
- ☑ The factories had canteens which provided relatively cheap food.
- ☑ Women with children could access childcare facilities in towns.
- ☑ Shock brigades, or workers who exceeded production targets, could earn more.

DID YOU KNOW?

At the time of the Bolshevik Revolution, less than one sixth of the population of Russia were industrial workers.

FAMILY LIFE, 1924-41

The USSR's social policies aimed to create a specific type of family that served the needs of the nation.

What was the Soviet Union's view on family?

The Soviet Union's view on the family changed over time, from a period of more experimentation in the 1920s to Stalin's *(p.64)* Great Retreat *(p.50)* in 1936 which promoted traditional family values.

What were the Soviet Union views on homosexuality and family?

The USSR's views on homosexuality changed over time in 3 key ways:

- ☑ When the new communist government rewrote the Criminal Codes in 1922 and 1926, they did not include any law which prohibited homosexuality, so it was therefore legal.
- ☑ Attitudes tended to be homophobic and homosexuals suffered verbal and physical abuse.
- ☑ Stalin's *(p.64)* government made homosexuality illegal again in 1933.

What was the Soviet Union view on abortion and family?

The USSR's attitude to abortion changed over time in 4 main ways.

- ✅ Abortion was made legal in 1917.
- ✅ Abortions were made illegal in 1936 in a bid to boost population growth and ensure the next generation of workers.
- ✅ Many women resorted to illegal, unregulated abortions as a result.
- ✅ Contraceptives were hard to obtain.

 What was the Soviet Union's view on working women and family?

Women were encouraged to work:

- ✅ There were 3 million women workers in the Soviet Union in 1928.
- ✅ This number had risen to more than 13 million by 1940.
- ✅ While around 40% of industrial workers were women, according to available figures, this still meant the majority of those employed in heavy industry were male.

 How did Stalin's Great Retreat impact the family in the Soviet Union?

Stalin's *(p.64)* Great Retreat *(p.50)* in 1936, promoted traditional family values in 3 main ways:

- ✅ Encouraging families to have children by offering financial rewards.
- ✅ Making abortion illegal.
- ✅ Making divorce more difficult and expensive. Stalin *(p.64)* believed marriage breakdown had led to abandoned children roaming the streets.

DID YOU KNOW?

Women bore the brunt of the consequences of the Soviet Union's social policies.

Theirs was a 'double burden' - many had both a full-time job and responsibility for the home.

COMMUNIST POLICIES ON WOMEN, 1924-1941

Communism holds that all people are equal. In reality, women never obtained equality with men.

 What was the communist view on women?

According to the theory of communism, all people are equal. Therefore, women should be treated equally to men. The Communist Party introduced a considerable amount of legislation to significantly improve women's rights; however, there were limitations in changing cultural attitudes and sexism still existed.

 What policies did the communists bring in to improve the legal rights of women?

After the October Revolution of 1917, the communists brought in 4 key policies to improve women's legal rights:

- ✅ 1917: Women and men were declared equal, women were given the right to vote and divorce was made easier.
- ✅ 1919: The Zhenotdel, a section of the Communist Party devoted to women's affairs headed by Alexandra Kollontai, was set up to improve their rights and position.
- ✅ 1920: Abortion was legalised.

☑ 1926: Women were able to own property separately from their husbands.

 ### What policies did the communists bring in to improve the education of women?

After the October Revolution of 1917, the communists brought in 3 main policies to improve education opportunities for women:

☑ In 1918, the Soviet Government issued a decree on education in which school was made compulsory for all children aged eight to 17.

☑ In 1929, 20% of higher education places were reserved for women.

☑ By 1940, over 40% of engineering students were women.

 ### What policies did the communists bring in to improve work for women?

After the October Revolution of 1917, the communists brought in 4 main policies to improve career opportunities for women:

☑ The law was changed to state men and women should be paid the same.

☑ Between 1918 and 1921, women were conscripted to work during the civil war to replace male workers.

☑ In 1923, Alexandra Kollontai became the world's first female ambassador, serving in Norway.

☑ By 1928, there were three million women workers. Stalin's *(p.64)* Five Year Plans and the rapid industrialisation of the USSR increased the number of women workers to over 13 million by 1940.

 ### What were the positive results for women because of communist policies?

There were 4 important positive results for women because of the policies introduced by the communist government:

☑ The legal changes did greatly improve the status of women, specifically for women in predominantly Muslim republics such as Azerbaijan.

☑ There were massive increases in the number of female workers during the civil war so there were greater job opportunities.

☑ Women were working in professions they had not been able to access before.

☑ Women were playing a greater role in politics and a few, but not many, did reach the higher levels of government.

 ### What were the limitations of communist policies for women?

Despite the communist government's policies for women, there were still 10 significant limitations:

☑ Changing their legal status did not change society's traditionally sexist views, meaning many women faced a double burden of working and completing all household tasks.

☑ In reality, women did not see equality in the workplace. They did not get promoted, faced sexism and only received about 2/3 of a man's wage.

☑ Some communist policies had a negative impact on women. For example, making divorce easier made many women's lives worse as 70% of divorces were initiated by men. Often a pregnant wife would be abandoned, leaving them as a single parent with no financial support.

☑ There were negative reactions to some communist policies. For example, the campaign for the unveiling of Muslim women led to violence and honour killings.

☑ There were still only a few women in important roles in the government, and in 1930 only 15% of the party membership were women.

☑ The Zhenotdel was closed down in 1930 as the communist government claimed equality had been achieved.

☑ Stalin's *(p.64)* Great Retreat *(p.50)* of 1936 meant there was a return to traditional family values. Under the 1936 Family Code, abortion was made illegal and divorce became more expensive.

☑ Stalin's *(p.64)* collectivisation policy had a terrible impact on women in the countryside as men migrated to towns and cities in search of work.

☑ Women in the countryside faced lower pay, lower standards of living and fewer services.

✅ By the 1950s, there was an imbalance between the genders in the countryside as the number of women vastly outnumbered men. This was largely due to the number of soldiers who had died in the Second World War.

DID YOU KNOW?

In 1925, Stalin proclaimed: 'Not a single great movement of the oppressed... has been able to do without the participation of working women.'

COMMUNIST POLICIES ON EDUCATION, 1924-1941

The communists inherited a country that could barely read or write.

❓ What was the communist view on education?

Education was important to the communists as a way to create a new, loyal generation with the right values. They wanted to create new 'Soviet men' and 'Soviet women'.

☭ What were the problems in the education system that the communists had to deal with?

There were 5 important problems the communists faced in education with the system they inherited from the tsarist regime:

✅ Many children did not attend school as they had to pay and could not afford it.

✅ There were not enough schools or teachers.

✅ Many schools were run by the Russian Orthodox Church and the communists were atheists; they did not believe in God.

✅ There was a lack of resources and supplies for schools as they were underfunded.

✅ There were very high levels of illiteracy. Approximately 65 million people were illiterate, and only 32% of the population could read and write in 1914.

☭ What education policies did the Communist Party introduce?

The communists brought in 6 main policies over time:

✅ A Commissariat of Education was set up in 1917. It promised free and compulsory education for all children aged seven to 17 and the expansion of university education.

✅ In 1918, the Soviet government issued a decree on education which nationalised all religious schools, banned corporal punishment, homework and exams, and established unified labour schools so that children aged seven to 17 received training for work.

✅ In 1919, the campaign for the 'liquidation of illiteracy' was introduced to end illiteracy. Rabfaki, or remedial schools, were set up to teach basic literacy and numeracy. All soldiers in the Red Army had to attend literacy classes.

✅ In 1929, the government introduced a quota system for working class students entry into university. This was to encourage working class students to attend.

✅ In 1930, Stalin *(p.64)* focused again on eliminating illiteracy and made primary school compulsory for all children up to the age of 12.

✅ In 1936, Stalin *(p.64)* reversed some of the early communist education policies because of the problems they created. In his Great Retreat *(p.50)*, he re-introduced traditional teaching methods and discipline, subjects and textbooks set by the government.

☭ How did Stalin control education in communist Russia?

There were 6 main ways in which Stalin *(p.64)* controlled education:

- ☑ In the Great Retreat *(p.50)* of the 1930s, he introduced stricter controls in education.
- ☑ The government provided official textbooks which had to be used. One example was 'The Short Course of the History of the All Union Communist Party' which glorified Stalin's *(p.64)* role in the revolution.
- ☑ The government controlled the curriculum and subjects such as Russian, communist ideology and science were made compulsory.
- ☑ There was very strict teacher discipline and students had to wear uniforms and sit in rows.
- ☑ All children had to attend school until the age of 15.
- ☑ Students were indoctrinated with socialist views at school and through the youth group, the Pioneers.

What were the results of the communist education policies?

There were 6 key effects of the communists' education policies:

- ☑ The initial changes of 1919 created problems as schools lacked discipline.
- ☑ Many children did not attend, especially in the countryside, or disappeared at harvest time.
- ☑ Schools were underfunded during the civil war and New Economic Policy period, and schools still charged fees.
- ☑ By 1928, about 60% of primary aged children were in school. By 1932, that had increased to 95%.
- ☑ The literacy drive was incredibly successful as 90% of Soviet adults attended a course. By 1939, over 94% of the population was literate.
- ☑ The policy of collectivisation and Stalin's *(p.64)* purges had a negative effect on education as teachers were attacked and removed from the workforce.

DID YOU KNOW?

All soldiers in the Red Army had to attend literacy classes.

COMMUNIST POLICIES ON FAMILY, 1924-1941

Communist family policies saw experimentation in the 1920s and a return to traditional values in the 1930s.

What was the communist view on family?

The communist view of family changed over time. Initially, they saw the traditional family as unnecessary and bourgeois. However, Stalin's *(p.64)* Great Retreat *(p.50)* in 1936 saw the return of more traditional views about family.

What policies on family did the communists introduce?

The communists brought in 4 main policies which affected the family:

- ☑ In 1918, the Family Code said the state would provide child care and social services as the family was no longer necessary. Divorce was made easier, abortion was legalised and crèches were made available.
- ☑ In 1927, new marriage laws meant that unregistered marriages and registered marriages had equal status.
- ☑ In 1936, Stalin *(p.64)* returned to traditional family values in his Great Retreat *(p.50)* which made divorce more expensive, and both male homosexuality and abortion were made illegal.
- ☑ In July 1944, the status of family was increased again, as a tax on single people was introduced and women who had ten or more children received the 'Mother Heroine' award.

What were the results of the communists' policies on family?

The communists' policies on family had mixed results:

- ☑ The initial policy of 1918 had unintended consequences because it encouraged divorce and family breakdown resulting in an increase in single mothers and abandoned children. By the mid-1920s the USSR had the highest divorce rate in Europe.
- ☑ It led to social problems with gangs of orphans roaming the streets.
- ☑ Stalin's *(p.64)* Great Retreat *(p.50)* led to a 28% increase in births from 1931 to 1940.

DID YOU KNOW?

One Soviet propaganda poster stated: 'Women have the right to vote and be elected equally with men. Hail the equality of Soviet women.'

COMMUNIST POLICIES ON ART AND CULTURE, 1924-1941

Art and culture were to re-enforce socialist views and help create new Soviet men and women.

What was the communist view on art and culture?

The Communist Party felt art and culture should create the 'new Soviet man' - an ideal socialist who thought and acted according to socialist values. This would completely remove and destroy the culture of tsarist Russia.

How was art and culture controlled under Bolshevik rule?

Under the communist government there was control in 3 main ways through censorship and propaganda:

- ☑ The Commissariat of Enlightenment was set up in 1917, under the leadership of Anatoly Lunacharsky, to support and encourage artists to work with the communist government. Initially, under Lenin, it allowed experimentation; under Stalin *(p.64)*, it was used to control artists.
- ☑ Banned books were removed from libraries and schools.
- ☑ All publications, including newspapers and magazines, had to be approved by the government censorship office.

What was the Proletkult movement in communist art and culture?

The Proletkult was:

- ☑ A movement supported by Anatoly Lunacharsky, the head of the Commissariat of Enlightenment, and Alexander Bogdanov.
- ☑ An attempt to create the USSR's own proletarian culture to promote communist values.
- ☑ It began in 1918 and was replaced by social realism under Stalin *(p.64)* from the 1930s.

What was the avant-garde movement in communist art and culture?

The avant-garde movement in art and culture:

- ☑ Challenged traditional art and encouraged experimentation.
- ☑ It included Modernism and Futurism - art that conveyed images of the future.
- ☑ It was a popular art movement after the First World War and saw avant-garde films created such as 'Battleship Potemkin' in 1925 by the director, Eisenstein.

What was socialist realism in communist art and culture?

Socialist realism *(p.39)*:

☑ Was a type of art which portrayed life under socialism in a positive way.

☑ Tended to portray ordinary people in ordinary situations, such as work, mines and schools, as heroes.

☑ Became the only acceptable form of art under Stalin's *(p.64)* rule from the 1930s onwards.

DID YOU KNOW?

The 1920s was a period of experimentation in Russian arts and culture.

Some of this experimentation did not work. One play, called 'Mystery Bouffe', was cancelled after 3 performances as the audience struggled to understand it.

COMMUNIST POLICIES ON RELIGION, 1924-1941

Communists are atheists.

 What was the communist view on religion?

Communists are atheists; they do not believe in religion. They saw it as a threat to communism because the Russian Orthodox Church had power, position and status.

 What was Lenin's view of religion in communist Russia?

Lenin was very anti-religion and pursued policies to remove the influence of the Church in the USSR.

What was Stalin's view on religion in communist Russia?

Stalin *(p.64)* was anti-religion and wanted to remove the influence of the Church in the USSR. However, he was more pragmatic than Lenin. During the Second World War he allowed the Church to have more influence to help the country.

How did the communists control religion?

The Communist Party brought in 4 main measures to control the Church and religion:

☑ In January 1918, the Decree Concerning Separation of Church and State was issued. This closed church schools, stopped state subsidies and nationalised church property.

☑ In 1918, the Decree on Freedom of Conscience separated the Church from state. The Church lost land, religious publications were banned, and religious education outside home was banned.

☑ There were attacks on priests and churches under Lenin and Stalin *(p.64)*. In Stalin's Great Purge, there were quotas for how many priests should be purged.

☑ During the Second World War, Stalin *(p.64)* relaxed the persecution of religion for pragmatic reasons to support people. Churches reopened to give comfort to families.

What was the communist attitude towards the Jewish religion?

Stalin's *(p.64)* treatment of Jews worsened over time in 6 main ways:

☑ All decrees which controlled religion affected Jewish people as well.

☑ After the Second World War, Stalin's *(p.64)* anti-Semitism grew and attacks increased.

☑ Jewish people were sacked from government posts and industry if they held any responsibility.

- ☑ There was a purge of Jewish leaders and some were executed.
- ☑ The government made it very difficult for Jewish people to emigrate to Israel.
- ☑ Many Jewish institutions such as schools were closed.

DID YOU KNOW?

Many beautiful Russian Orthodox churches were destroyed or used for other purposes.

For example, the beautiful cathedral of Christ the Saviour in Moscow was demolished to make way for a new 'Palace of the Soviets'. This new building was cancelled due to the outbreak of the Second World War and the site was then used for a swimming pool. At that time, it was the biggest in the world!

STALIN'S GREAT RETREAT

The Great Retreat was a period when social policies promoted a traditional agenda.

What was the Great Retreat?

The Great Retreat was a policy introduced by Stalin *(p.64)* in the USSR which promoted traditional family values.

When was the Great Retreat?

The Great Retreat occurred during the 1930s.

Why did Stalin introduce the Great Retreat?

The Great Retreat of the 1930s was introduced because due to 4 main reasons:

- ☑ It was a reaction to the perceived failures of the government's policies on the family and women of the 1920s.
- ☑ The birth rate had dropped.
- ☑ Family breakdown had increased causing social problems.
- ☑ It was felt that there was a breakdown in discipline in education and of the youth.

How did the Great Retreat affect families?

There were 5 key changes that affected family life because of the Great Retreat:

- ☑ Parents could be fined if their child was in trouble with the authorities.
- ☑ Divorce was discouraged by increasing the cost from 4 to 50 roubles and forcing couples to attend court.
- ☑ Divorced fathers had to pay child maintenance. If they did not pay they could be jailed for up to two years.
- ☑ Male homosexuality was made illegal.
- ☑ Abortion was made illegal to encourage larger families.

How did the Great Retreat affect education?

In the Great Retreat, Stalin *(p.64)* re-introduced exams, homework, traditional teaching methods and subjects, and textbooks set by the government. School became much more strict as tighter discipline was re-introduced.

What was the impact of the Great Retreat?

The Great Retreat had 3 main effects:

- ☑ It had a negative effect on women. It promoted traditional family values which restricted many of the new opportunities women had in the 1920s.
- ☑ The birth rate increased temporarily.
- ☑ The divorce rate decreased.

DID YOU KNOW?

The USSR in the 1920s witnessed some social experimentation.

However, there was always tension with some Communist Party members and sections of society which held traditional views.

ETHNIC GROUPS

The Soviet Union treated ethnic groups harshly.

What was the persecution of ethnic minorities in the Soviet Union?

Ethnic minorities were treated as a potential threat to Stalin's *(p.64)* position and the communist government. Therefore, they were persecuted and were treated with hostility.

When did the persecution of ethnic minorities in the USSR take place?

The persecution of ethnic minorities increased in the 1930s and continued until Stalin's *(p.64)* death in 1953.

Why did the persecution of ethnic minorities in the USSR take place?

There were 3 main reasons why ethnic minorities were persecuted:

- ☑ The USSR was made up of many different nationalities. Many of these had distinct identities and wanted independence from the Soviet Union. They were therefore seen as a threat to unity.
- ☑ Stalin *(p.64)* blamed specific nationalities for the resistance to collectivisation. Some believe that is why he failed to help the Ukrainians during the famine of 1932.
- ☑ Stalin *(p.64)* believed that because some nationalities wanted independence, they could not be trusted when the Soviet Union was under threat of invasion or at war.

What happened to ethnic minorities in the USSR during the persecution?

There were 6 different ways in which ethnic minorities were persecuted:

- ☑ All 15 republics of the USSR had to suppress their local culture and language.
- ☑ All schools had to teach Russian *(p.46)* and loyalty to the USSR.
- ☑ During the purges between 1936 and 1938, many national leaders, teachers and writers were arrested and either executed or imprisoned in the gulags.
- ☑ Whole national groups were moved or deported to different areas in the USSR. For example, when Nazi Germany invaded in 1941, all Germans in the Volga area were rounded up and exiled to either central Asia or Siberia.
- ☑ The Second World War led to an increase in purges of ethnic groups during the war, and after it had ended, as Stalin *(p.64)* became increasingly paranoid. For example, there were mass deportations of Lithuanians, Estonians and Latvians.
- ☑ The last major attack on an ethnic group was the Mingrelian Affair in 1951, in which a purge began in Georgia aimed at the leader of the NKVD *(p.34)*, Lavrentiy Beria, who was also Mingrelian.

THE NAZI-SOVIET PACT, 1939

Many observers were sceptical about the pact between Hitler and Stalin. Cartoon captions created at the time include: 'Strange bedfellows', 'Wonder how long the honeymoon will last?', and 'Someone is taking someone for a walk'.

What was the Nazi-Soviet Pact

The Nazi-Soviet Pact was a non-aggression pact between Soviet Russia and Nazi Germany. It was also known as the Molotov-Ribbentrop Pact.

When was the Nazi-Soviet Pact signed?

The Nazi-Soviet Pact was signed in late August 1939.

What did the Nazi-Soviet Pact say?

The Nazi-Soviet Pact contained two main agreements between the USSR and Germany.

- ☑ Germany and the USSR agreed not to go to war, even though both sides knew that war between them was inevitable
- ☑ They secretly agreed to partition Polish territory between them.

Why did Germany sign the Nazi-Soviet Pact?

Germany had a number of reasons for signing the Nazi-Soviet Pact.

- ☑ Hitler didn't want to meet opposition from the USSR while Germany invaded Poland.
- ☑ He didn't want to enter a war on two fronts, in which Germany fought the USSR in the east and Britain and France in the west. This was a mistake made in the First World War - German troops were divided between two fronts and this weakened their army.
- ☑ He wanted to deal with the threat from Britain and France and secure the Polish territory before entering into a war with the USSR.

Why did Russia sign the Nazi-Soviet Pact?

Stalin *(p.64)* was aware of Hitler's intentions and knew their two countries would end up at war. However, in 1939 the Nazi-Soviet Pact suited his short-term ambitions.

- ☑ He mistrusted the western powers like Britain and France and didn't believe they would protect the USSR from Germany, especially after the Soviet Union was excluded from the Munich Conference.
- ☑ He hoped that war between Germany, Britain and France would give the USSR time to build up its army and strengthen its defences.
- ☑ He hoped to gain Polish territory, much of which had been taken from Russia at the end of the First World War.
- ☑ He also viewed the Allies as weak because of the policy of appeasement.

What was the significance of the Nazi-Soviet Pact?

The Nazi-Soviet Pact had a number of results including:

- ☑ It caused shock and consternation, especially in Britain and France. They had hoped the Soviet threat would prevent Germany from invading Poland.
- ☑ It meant Germany was confident about invading Poland, especially as Britain and France had so far presented no threat.
- ☑ On 1st September 1939, Germany invaded Poland. This was an immediate cause of the Second World War.

How did Britain and France react to the Nazi-Soviet Pact?

The Nazi-Soviet Pact had huge implications for Britain and France, both of whom were stunned by the news.

- ☑ This was a blow for Britain and France, and Chamberlain was blamed for Stalin *(p.64)* choosing to side with Hitler. Opinion polls showed 84% of the British population had hoped for an alliance with the USSR.
- ☑ It had been previously believed that only the USSR could protect Poland from Hitler. The pact was a huge blow to the Polish.
- ☑ However, at the time there was a great mistrust of the communist Soviet Union, which helps to explain why Chamberlain didn't pursue an alliance with them more aggressively.

When did the Nazi-Soviet Pact end?

It remained in effect for almost two years. It was broken by the Germans when they invaded the USSR on 22nd June, 1941.

DID YOU KNOW?

Although Hitler signed the non-aggression pact with Stalin in order to achieve his foreign policy goal of destroying communism, Germany later invaded Russia in 1941.

THE NAZI INVASION OF THE USSR, 1941

Operation Barbarossa, Operation Red Beard, was the Nazi invasion of the USSR.

What was the Nazi invasion of the USSR?

Nazi Germany launched a campaign called Operation Barbarossa to invade the Soviet Union.

When was the Nazi invasion of the USSR?

The Nazi invasion of the USSR began on 22nd June, 1941.

What happened during the initial Nazi invasion of the USSR?

The 4 key events of the initial invasion were:

- ☑ The German Army was split into three different Army Groups which attacked the USSR in the north, the centre, and the south along the Soviet-Polish border.
- ☑ Army Group North moved towards Leningrad and began their siege of the city.
- ☑ Army Group Centre moved east to Minsk, Smolensk and Moscow.
- ☑ Army Group South aimed for the Ukraine and, after taking Kiev, headed to Kharkov.

Why did the Soviet Union suffer from setbacks during the initial Nazi invasion of the USSR?

There are 5 key reasons why the Soviet Union suffered setbacks during the initial Nazi invasion between 1941 and 1942:

- ☑ Stalin (p.64) was not expecting the Nazi invasion, despite being warned that the Nazis were preparing to invade.
- ☑ Stalin (p.64) failed to provide leadership during the first week of the invasion by isolating himself. Either he was suffering from shock or he was avoiding being overthrown, but it left the Red Army without clear direction.
- ☑ The Red Army had been weakened by Stalin's (p.64) Great Purge of 1936-38, because the most experienced officers had been killed.
- ☑ Nazi tactics were very effective at pushing the Soviet troops back. 'Blitzkrieg' or lightning war deployed tanks, the air force and ground troops in combination, enabled the Germans to advance very quickly. The German Army was also very large.
- ☑ The German Army could encircle and capture the Red Army because of Stalin's (p.64) order to not retreat.

What was the extent of the setbacks that the USSR suffered during the initial part of the Nazi invasion of the Soviet Union?

By the end of the initial Nazi invasion of the USSR, the USSR had suffered in the following 3 key ways:

- ☑ 45% of the Russian population was under Nazi occupation.
- ☑ Lost vital farming areas and suffered a reduction in production of supplies for the war.
- ☑ 3 million soldiers were captured.

How did the Soviet Union survive the Nazi invasion of the USSR?

There were 4 main reasons that helped the USSR survive the invasion:

- ☑ Factories and people were physically moved to the east of the Ural mountains to protect them from German attacks. Stalin (p.64) implemented a scorched earth policy, so what was left was burnt to prevent the Germans from using it.
- ☑ The start of the Nazi invasion was delayed, and therefore, they faced difficult winter conditions before they could take Moscow and Leningrad. They were not prepared for the freezing cold.
- ☑ Propaganda, centred around Stalin (p.64), motivated the people to keep working and fighting.
- ☑ When the Red Army counter-attacked in December 1941, they were very successful and pushed the Nazi German Army back from Moscow.

Why was the Soviet Union successful in the end against the Nazi invasion of the USSR?

There were 6 main reasons why the USSR finally defeated the Nazis:

- ☑ They received around $11 billion of military equipment, as well as food and vital transport such as trains, from the Allies.
- ☑ Between 1942 and 1943, the Soviets produced aircraft and other arms much faster than the Germans as it spent so much on its war economy.
- ☑ Stalin (p.64) was a very good wartime leader setting up the Soviet High Command or STAVKA. He followed the advice from very able generals such as Zhukov, whereas Hitler made some very poor military decisions in his war with the USSR.
- ☑ The Battle of Stalingrad (p.56) proved to be a disaster for Nazi Germany, because they lost the whole of the elite Sixth Army.
- ☑ The people of the Soviet Union rose to the challenge. Through sheer hard work and endurance of enormous suffering (starvation, lack of power etc), they supported the Soviet war effort.
- ☑ There were harsh punishments for civilians and soldiers if they did not perform. Workers who were late to work could be imprisoned and soldiers that refused to fight could be shot.

STALIN'S LEADERSHIP

Stalin's leadership of the USSR went through many stages.

How was Stalin as a leader?

How Stalin *(p.64)* was viewed as a leader changed over time. It depended on what was happening at the time and his policies.

What kind of leader was Stalin before the Second World War?

Before the Second World War, Stalin *(p.64)* created a personal dictatorship using 3 main methods:

- ☑ Expanding the system of terror, established under Lenin, allowed Stalin *(p.64)* to eliminate his enemies both inside the Party and external to the Party.
- ☑ He used the NKVD *(p.34)*, Gulags, and his absolute control of art and culture, education and the media to crush all opposition.
- ☑ Pushing through the policies of collectivisation and industrialisation in the USSR *(p.20)* to control all aspects of the economy.

What kind of leader was Stalin during the Second World War?

Stalin *(p.64)* was seen as good wartime leader because of 4 main reasons:

- ☑ He dedicated the economy to the war effort - over 50% of the national income was spent on fighting the war.
- ☑ He set up the STAVKA, the Soviet High Command, to lead the war effort and listened to experienced military advisers.
- ☑ He reopened Orthodox churches - a very popular move - so that people had emotional support during the war.
- ☑ The USSR defeated Nazi Germany in 1945.

What kind of leader was Stalin after the Second World War?

How Stalin *(p.64)* was seen as a leader changed between 1945 and 1953:

- ☑ The years between 1945 and 1953 are known as the period of 'high Stalinism'.
- ☑ Stalin *(p.64)* is perceived as having total control as he increased the use of terror, and launched a crackdown on art and culture.
- ☑ However, by 1949, Stalin *(p.64)* was becoming weak. His authority was coming under threat from a new generation of Communist Party members, including Beria and Malenkov.

THE BATTLE OF STALINGRAD, 1942

The Battle of Stalingrad was eventually won by the USSR. However, the cost was enormous.

What was the Battle of Stalingrad?

The Battle of Stalingrad was the largest confrontation of the Second World War between Nazi Germany and the USSR.

When was the Battle of Stalingrad?

The Battle of Stalingrad lasted from 23rd August, 1942, until 2nd February, 1943.

Why did the Nazis begin the Battle of Stalingrad?

The German 6th Army, led by General Friedrich von Paulus, wanted to take command of Stalingrad so they could provide supplies to their armies in the south. In particular, the Nazis wanted oil from Baku, in Azerbaijan.

What were the main events of the Battle of Stalingrad?

There were 6 key events of the Battle of Stalingrad:

- ☑ The German Army attacked in June 1942, and reached the outskirts of Stalingrad in August.
- ☑ The German Army used tanks to try to push through to the Volga River. This did not work very well in the bombed out city.
- ☑ The Red Army responded with night attacks, snipers and close combat.
- ☑ The German attack had ground to a halt by November 1942.
- ☑ The Red Army launched their counter-attack, Operation Uranus, on 19th November. They attacked Nazi Germany's allies in the north and the south of the city. Nazi Germany's allies collapsed.
- ☑ General von Paulus, the commander of the Sixth Army, surrendered to the Soviets on 31st January, 1943.

How did the Soviets respond at the Battle of Stalingrad?

The Soviets responded in the following 4 main ways:

- ☑ The Red Army used a tactic called 'fighting retreat'.
- ☑ This is a planned retreat, where a force can still fight, while falling back to a more pragmatic position.
- ☑ This put a strain on supply lines to the German Army.
- ☑ Stalin *(p.64)* forbade an evacuation of Stalingrad to prevent the Germans from taking it over.

How did the Germans react to the Battle of Stalingrad?

There were 2 main reactions of the German Army:

- ☑ The Germans were surprised by how the Soviets fought back, as they had never faced such determined resistance.
- ☑ The Soviet forces were strong, and the Germans were not prepared for the harshness of the winter.

Why was the Battle of Stalingrad significant?

The Battle of Stalingrad was significant for 5 main reasons:

☑ It massively boosted the morale of the USSR and reputation of Stalin *(p.64)*, because it was Nazi Germany's first major defeat in Europe.

☑ It was a turning point because after the battle the German Army slowly retreated back to Germany.

☑ Nazi Germany lost a vast amount of soldiers and equipment with approximately 500,000 soldiers either dead, injured or captured.

☑ It shattered the Sixth Army which was an elite part of the German Army.

☑ The human cost for the Soviet Union was horrific with 500,000 soldiers dead, and about 800,000 civilians dead from starvation, the cold or bombs.

DID YOU KNOW?

The fighting was ferocious. It is reported that some survivors committed suicide afterwards, suffering from what today would be recognised as post-traumatic stress disorder.

THE SOVIET INVASION OF GERMANY

The tide was turned against the Nazis when the USSR invaded Germany in 1945.

What was the Soviet invasion of Germany?

The Soviet invasion of Germany occurred in the last few years of the Second World War from 1944 to 1945.

What happened during the Soviet invasion of Germany?

There were 6 main events that occurred:

☑ In July 1943, the Germans launched an attack on the USSR army at Kursk, in Russia, which failed and the Germans began to retreat to Germany.

☑ In June 1944, the Soviet Union launched an attack on Germany.

☑ In July 1944, the Soviets recaptured Minsk, in Belarus, and began their invasion of Poland.

☑ In January 1945, the Red Army invaded Warsaw.

☑ In April 1945, the Red Army captured Vienna. From there they could march into Germany, by April 1945.

☑ By the end of April 1945, the army broke through into Berlin.

Why did Germany surrender after the Soviet invasion?

Germany surrendered because:

☑ By spring 1945, the Soviets were approaching Berlin from the east and the Western Allies were approaching the city from the west.

☑ Hitler committed suicide because he knew defeat was imminent.

☑ Karl Dönitz, Hitler's successor, surrendered to the Allies on 7th May, 1945.

THE IMPACT OF THE SECOND WORLD WAR ON THE USSR

The damaging effects of the war on the USSR.

What problems did the Second World War cause for the USSR?

The Second World War, known as the Great Patriotic War in the USSR, caused political, economic and social problems for the USSR.

What was the political impact of the Second World War on the USSR?

Due to Second World War, or the Great Patriotic War, the government of the USSR increased its political control over the country and all aspects of life were subject to harsh controls.

What was the social impact of the Second World War on the USSR?

The Second World War had 4 main social impacts on the USSR:

- ☑ Around 20 million people were killed.
- ☑ More Soviet soldiers died defending Stalingrad *(p.56)* than the total number of US soldiers killed during their country's involvement in the war.
- ☑ 2,000 towns and cities were destroyed, along with 7,000 villages.
- ☑ 6 million houses were wrecked.

What was the economic impact of the Second World War on the USSR?

The Second World War had 3 main economic impacts on the USSR:

- ☑ Around 100,000 collective farms were destroyed.
- ☑ There were food shortages during and after the war due to the lack of men, working machinery and limited harvests.
- ☑ Industrial output of the USSR did not return to its 1940 levels until almost a decade after the war.

Quizzes, amazing exam preparation tools and more at GCSEHistory.com

FOURTH FIVE YEAR PLAN, 1946 TO 1950

The Fourth Five Year Plan focused on repairing the damage caused by the Second World War.

What was the Soviet Union's Fourth Five Year Plan?

The Fourth Five Year Plan was the fourth industrial plan created by Gosplan *(p.23)* for the USSR. It was a reaction to the damage caused by the Second World War.

When was the Fourth Five Year Plan in the Soviet Union?

The Fourth Five Year Plan was from 1946 to 1950.

What were the aims of the Fourth Five Year Plan in the Soviet Union?

The Fourth Five Year Plan was aimed at reconstruction, following the devastation caused by the Second World War. It was still focused on heavy industry.

What impact did the Second World War have on the Soviet Union that the Fourth Five Year Plan had to address?

The Second World War had a devastating effect on the USSR in 4 main ways:

- ✅ 5 million homes were destroyed.
- ✅ 100,000 collective farms were destroyed.
- ✅ 65,000km of railway was destroyed.
- ✅ 19 million civilians were killed.

What were the successes of the Fourth Five Year Plan in the Soviet Union?

The Third Five Year Plan had 4 main successes:

- ✅ Production of consumer goods doubled from 12% to 24%.
- ✅ Industrial production in electricity, pig iron and coal surpassed pre-war levels.
- ✅ 2.5 million people were rehoused.
- ✅ The USSR could exploit resources in eastern Europe to help its recovery.

What were the weaknesses of the Fourth Five Year Plan in the Soviet Union?

The Fourth Five Year Plan had 4 key weaknesses:

- ✅ The supply of consumer goods remained insufficient.
- ✅ Workers were worse off as there were pay cuts and the rouble was devalued by 90%.
- ✅ Lack of housing was still a major issue.
- ✅ Farming took a very long time to recover. It took until 1952 for grain production to reach pre-war levels due to the lack of men, investment and machinery.

DID YOU KNOW?

The rebuilding of the USSR was a remarkable achievement.
Although its people suffered due to the lack of consumer goods.

STALIN'S LEGACY

Stalin had an enormous impact, both domestically and in international relations.

What was Stalin's legacy for the USSR?

Stalin's *(p.64)* legacy was considerable for both the USSR itself and its position and status in the world.

What was Stalin's legacy for the USSR in the world?

Stalin's *(p.64)* legacy for the USSR as a world power was considerable:

- ☑ The USSR was a superpower with nuclear capabilities that the West feared so much they created NATO, a defensive military alliance.
- ☑ He had enabled the USSR to industrialise so that its economy now rivaled the American economy.
- ☑ Eastern Europe had been taken over, converted to communism and the countries had become satellite states to the USSR.
- ☑ The USSR had become so powerful it was able to offer aid to other countries such as North Korea and North Vietnam in an attempt to spread communism.

What was Stalin's legacy for the USSR at home?

Stalin's *(p.64)* legacy for the USSR was considerable:

- ☑ His economic policies industrialised the USSR, but failed to provide basic consumer goods for his people.
- ☑ He created a personalised dictatorship in which opposition of any kind was eliminated using a cruel system of terror, Gulags, and censorship controlled by the secret police.
- ☑ He encouraged a return to traditional values. Policies on the family, women and education all pushed traditional values.
- ☑ People's life experience in the USSR depended on who you were and where you lived. Peasants in the countryside suffered the worst living standards with low pay, a lack of access to services and no freedom of movement. Top Party officials, in comparison, lived in luxury.
- ☑ Stalin *(p.64)* was seen as a heroic leader because of his cult of personality *(p.37)*, but also feared because of the system of terror.

DID YOU KNOW?

Stalin's eldest child, a soldier in the Red Army, was captured during the Second World War and died in Sachsenhausen concentration camp in 1943.

LEV KAMENEV

Lev Kamenev was considered a rival by Stalin.

Who was Kamenev?

Lev Kamenev was from a working class family. He joined the Bolshevik Party and became a leading member of the Party. He became a close friend of Lenin and spent time with him in exile.

When did Kamenev join the Communist Party?

Kamenev joined the Bolshevik Party in 1903.

What was Lenin's relationship with Kamenev?

Kamenev was a close friend of Lenin's, but had opposed his plan for a revolution in October 1917.

What were Kamenev's political beliefs?

Kamenev was on the left of the Communist Party. He believed in permanent or world-wide revolution and was against the New Economic Policy, NEP *(p. 18)*.

What did Lenin say about Kamenev in his 'Testament'?

Lenin criticised Kamenev for not supporting him in the October Revolution of 1917 in his 'Testament'.

What roles did Kamenev have in the Communist Party?

Kamenev held 4 key positions of responsibility:

- ☑ He was in charge of the Communist Party in Petrograd when he returned from exile in March 1917.
- ☑ In 1919, he became the leader of the Communist Party in Moscow.
- ☑ Between March 1921 and 1926, he was a full member of the Politburo.
- ☑ When Lenin died in 1924, he was the acting head of the communist government.

What happened to Kamenev during the leadership struggle with Stalin?

In 1925, Stalin *(p. 64)* allied with Kamenev and Zinoviev to defeat Trotsky. Between 1927 and 1929 Stalin turned against Kamenev and allied with Bukharin.

What happened to Kamenev in the Great Purges?

Stalin *(p. 64)* viewed Kamenev as a threat so was targeted in the Great Purges of 1936 to 1938:

- ☑ He was arrested and put on trial during the Trial of the Sixteen in 1936 with Zinoviev.
- ☑ He was accused of the murder of Kirov, plotting to overthrow the government and sabotaging the Five Year Plans.
- ☑ Kamenev confessed to the crimes of which he was accused to save the lives of his family. He was executed by being shot.

When did Kamenev die?

Kamenev was executed after his show trial on 24th August, 1936. He was shot.

DID YOU KNOW?

3 facts about Kamenev:

- ✔ He did not finish his university education because he was thrown out as he demonstrated against the tsar.
- ✔ He was married to Leon Trotsky's sister, Olga, and they had two children.
- ✔ Although he confessed to save his family, his wife and sons were shot.

SERGEI KIROV

Stalin saw Sergei Kirov as a threat to his position as party leader.

Who was Kirov?

Sergei Kirov joined the Communist Party in 1904 and participated in the 1905 Revolution, the October 1917 Revolution and the Civil War. He became a leading member of the Communist Party and the government of the Soviet Union in the 1930s.

What roles did Kirov have in the Communist Party?

Kirov held 3 key positions of responsibility in the Communist Party and the government of the USSR:

- ☑ In 1921, he was appointed the head of the Azerbaijan Communist Party.
- ☑ In 1926, Kirov was appointed as the head of the Leningrad Communist Party.
- ☑ Kirov was a member of the Politburo from July 1930 to his death in 1934.

Why did Kirov's relationship with Stalin deteriorate?

Kirov's relationship with Stalin *(p.64)* deteriorated for 5 main reasons:

- ☑ Kirov was popular and charismatic so Stalin *(p.64)* saw him as an opponent.
- ☑ In 1932, Kirov voted with others in the Politburo against the execution of Ryutin. Ryutin had criticised Stalin's *(p.64)* policies of industrialisation and collectivisation in a 200 page article .
- ☑ During the 17th Party Congress, Kirov was given a standing ovation that was longer than the applause for Stalin *(p.64)* .
- ☑ During the 17th Party Congress, Kirov made critical comments about the effects of industrialisation and collectivisation.
- ☑ He received more votes than Stalin *(p.64)* for a position on the Central Committee.

When was Kirov murdered?

Kirov was assassinated by being shot in the back of the neck on 1st December, 1934 by Leonid Nikolayev.

Why was Kirov's murder significant?

Kirov was significant due to 3 key reasons:

- ☑ He challenged Stalin's *(p.64)* position of power as shown by events during the 17th Party Congress.
- ☑ Stalin *(p.64)* realised that he was not completely secure in his position as leader.
- ☑ It is likely that Stalin *(p.64)* organised the assassination of Kirov as an excuse to begin the purges.

DID YOU KNOW?

The circumstances of Sergei Kirov's murder were very suspicious.

Leonid Nikolayev, his assassin, managed to slip past the guards of the Smolny Institute where Kirov worked and shoot him.

Quizzes, amazing exam preparation tools and more at GCSEHistory.com

VLADIMIR LENIN

Lenin was the first leader of the USSR as well as its founder.

Who was Lenin?

Lenin was the leader of the Russian Communist Party and the USSR. He developed the political theory of Marxism-Leninism. His full name was Vladimir Ilyich Ulyanov.

When did Lenin join the Communist Party?

Lenin joined the Communist Party in 1903 and became the leader of the USSR after the October Revolution of 1917 until his death in 1924.

Where was Lenin during the February Revolution?

Lenin was in exile in Switzerland. This meant he did not play a part in the February Revolution.

When did Lenin return to Russia?

Lenin returned to Russia on 3rd April, 1917 but fled to Finland in July 1917. He returned again on 10th October, 1917.

Why did Lenin return to Russia?

Lenin was helped by the Germans to return to Russia. The Germans wanted to cause unrest in Russia in the hope the country would pull out of the First World War. They believed Lenin would cause that unrest.

What were Lenin's April theses?

Lenin's manifesto, his 'April Theses' had 4 main demands.

- ☑ Peace: He demanded that Russia pull out of the war.
- ☑ Bread: Lenin claimed the Bolsheviks could solve the food shortages.
- ☑ Land: Lenin wanted land to be given to the peasants and to end the social hierarchies that had existed under the tsar.
- ☑ All power to the Soviets: Lenin demanded all cooperation with the Provisional Government and any other party should end, and all power should be with the Soviets.

What was Lenin's 'State and Revolution' pamphlet about?

The 'State and Revolution' pamphlet was:

- ☑ Written by Lenin while he was in Finland.
- ☑ Stated that after taking power in a revolution, there would be a period of rule known as the ' dictatorship of the proletariat'.
- ☑ Its aim would be to create stability in the nation before the transition to full communism.

What part did Lenin play in the Sovnarkom?

Lenin did the following on the Sovnarkom, or the Council of People's Commissars:

- ☑ He was its chairman.
- ☑ He used the Sovnarkom to develop a dictatorship, rather than Russia becoming a genuinely equal socialist society.

When did Lenin die?

Lenin died on 21st January 1924 after suffering three strokes; the first in May 1922, the second in December 1922 and the final one in March 1923.

Who were Lenin's potential successors?

After Lenin's death in 1924, there was a power struggle over who would succeed him:

☑ There were several potential leaders - Stalin *(p.64)*, Trotsky, Kamenev, Zinoviev and Bukharin.

☑ Each candidate had their own strengths: Stalin *(p.64)* was general secretary of the Communist Party, Trotsky had led the Red Army, and Zinoviev and Kamenev had led the party in Petrograd and Moscow.

Who succeeded Lenin?

By 1929, Stalin *(p.64)* emerged as leader of the Communist Party and of the country.

How did Lenin's successor become leader?

There were 2 main methods Stalin *(p.64)* used to become Lenin's successor:

☑ He manipulated his rivals, who were also competing to become leader of the party, so he was able to remove them as competitors.

☑ He appeared to be the most moderate candidate and rose above the arguments and egos of his rivals.

What were Lenin's achievements?

Lenin was the communist leader of Russia and the USSR between 1917 and 1924. He achieved 7 important things:

☑ He adapted Karl Marx's theory of communism to create Marxism-Leninism. This was a theory on how to achieve a communist society in Russia in a shorter period of time than Marxism would allow.

☑ He created the 'April Theses' which enabled the Bolsheviks to get their message across more easily and gained them more support.

☑ He had led a successful communist revolution in Russia in October 1917.

☑ He led the Bolsheviks to victory in the Russian Civil War.

☑ He introduced War Communism which centralised Bolshevik control of the economy, increased centralisation of the party and enabled them win the civil war.

☑ He ended Russia's war with Germany through the Treaty of Brest-Litovsk in March 1918.

☑ He created a one-party state or a dictatorship.

DID YOU KNOW?

3 facts about Lenin:

✓ Lenin's older brother, Alexander, was executed for attempting to assassinate Tsar Alexander III.

✓ Lenin trained as a lawyer.

✓ Lenin's body was embalmed to preserve it and people can visit his mausoleum in Moscow's Red Square.

JOSEPH STALIN

Joseph Stalin was the brutal dictator of the USSR from 1929 to 1953.

Who was Joseph Stalin?

Joseph Stalin was a communist revolutionary from Georgia who was a member of the Communist Party and became the leader of the Soviet Union.

When did Stalin join the Communist Party?

Stalin joined the Communist Party in 1903. He was the leader of the USSR from the mid-1920s until his death in 1953.

What was Stalin's role in the Communist Party?

Stalin had 3 main positions in the Communist Party:

- ☑ In January 1912, Stalin was a member of the first Central Committee of the Bolshevik Party.
- ☑ He became the Commissar for Nationalities between 1917 and 1923 and was appointed the Commissar for State Control from 1919 to 1923.
- ☑ In 1922, Stalin was appointed the general secretary of the party's Central Committee.

Why was Stalin able to become the leader of the USSR?

There were 5 main reasons why Stalin became the leader of the USSR:

- ☑ He was a very clever politician who exploited the weaknesses of his rivals.
- ☑ His policies, such as socialism in one country, were more popular than Trotsky's policies.
- ☑ He used his power within the Communist Party as general secretary to put his own supporters into important posts to build his own power base.
- ☑ He turned circumstances to his advantage, such as using Lenin's funeral to undermine Trotsky.
- ☑ He played his rivals against one another so they undermined each other.

What happened during the purges under Stalin?

Stalin initiated 3 main purges at different times:

- ☑ The Great Purge occurred between 1936 and 1938. Old Bolsheviks and all those suspected of being an 'enemy of the people' were targeted. Essentially, this meant anyone who posed a threat to Stalin, real or imagined.
- ☑ During the Second World War, different nationalities were targeted, such as the Volga Germans and ethnic Finns, as their loyalty was considered suspect.
- ☑ After the Second World War, different groups such as Jews, Russian soldiers who had been German prisoners of war and the Leningrad Communist Party were purged.

What was Stalin's influence on education?

Stalin influenced education in three specific ways:

- ☑ The government decided what the school curriculum would be and what subjects would be taught. All schools taught sciences, Russian and communist ideology.
- ☑ The textbooks had to be approved by the government and must contain the 'correct' facts.
- ☑ The new textbooks rewrote history and praised Stalin as Lenin's loyal follower. The core curriculum was shaped according to Stalin's world view with the aim of creating new 'Soviet men' and 'Soviet women'.

How did art and culture in the Soviet Union develop under Stalin's rule?

Art and culture was controlled by the Soviet government in 3 key ways:

- ☑ The government had complete control over information and propaganda through the Commissariat of Enlightenment. This included all art and culture.
- ☑ Socialist realism *(p. 39)* was the regime's official art form. Its artists included Kuzma Petrov-Vodkin, Isaak Brodsky, Alexander Samokhvalov and Yuri Pimenov.
- ☑ Socialist realist art work was easy to understand and focused on workers in everyday situations. These workers were depicted as the heroes of Soviet society. The same rules applied to novels and music.

What was Stalin's view on Christianity?

The communists, as atheists, opposed the Russian Orthodox Church. Many churches were shut down and their priests imprisoned and even shot. Only 500 churches remained open by 1941, a reduction of almost 50,000 since the beginning of the First World War.

How did Stalin's regime treat Muslims?

Stalin oppressed Muslims using 4 main strategies:

- ☑ The use of Arabic writing was frowned upon and many non-Russian speakers were 're-educated' to speak Russian.
- ☑ Muslim schools and places of worship were closed down.
- ☑ Participating in the Hajj pilgrimage to Mecca was forbidden.
- ☑ The Soviet government organised unveiling of women campaigns.

How did Stalin's regime treat Judaism?

With regard to Judaism, anti-Semitism was illegal but many religious Jews were discriminated against. Stalin wanted to move all Jews to a designated region in the east called the Jewish Autonomous Oblast, but this idea failed.

Was the media censored under Stalin's regime?

The media had to be supportive of Stalin and the Communist Party. Works written by those who had been purged were banned, including Trotsky's. Economic data was also censored, which meant no one could check the claims of the government about the economy.

What were Joseph Stalin's beliefs?

Stalin believed in one-party rule. He was also convinced that the West wanted to destroy communism.

What conferences did Stalin attend?

Stalin attended the Tehran, Yalta and Potsdam conferences, which were discussions on Nazi Germany and how to end the war.

What was Stalin's involvement in the Cold War?

Stalin did not trust the West. His poor relationship with President Truman especially led to a deterioration in US-Soviet relations.

When did Stalin die?

Stalin died of a stroke on 5th March, 1953.

DID YOU KNOW?

3 facts about Stalin:
- ✔ His alias, Stalin, meant 'Man of Steel'.
- ✔ He committed bank robberies to help fund communist activities.
- ✔ He had been sent to a seminary to study as a priest when younger.

Quizzes, amazing exam preparation tools and more at GCSEHistory.com

LEON TROTSKY

Leon Trotsky was the architect of the Red Army's success in the Russian Civil War.

Who was Trotsky?

Leon Trotsky was a Soviet revolutionary, Marxist theorist, and politician. Trotsky was a brilliant orator - he was much more charismatic than Stalin *(p.64)*. He had worked closely with Lenin as the war commissar, commander of the Red Army.

Where was Trotsky during the February Revolution?

Trotsky had been in the USA during the February Revolution. In May 1917, after the February Revolution, he returned to Russia.

What did Trotsky believe in?

Trotsky believed in 'permanent revolution'. His argument was that the revolution would degenerate if it could not spread and become international. He thought the Bolsheviks should use instability around the world to spark revolutions elsewhere. This brought him into conflict with Stalin *(p.64)*. Stalin believed in 'Socialism in One Country'.

What were Trotsky's main roles?

Trotsky had 4 key roles:

- ☑ He was elected president of the Petrograd Soviet on 25th September 1917, because the Bolsheviks had protected Petrograd from the Kornilov Revolt.
- ☑ Trotsky played a key role in the October Revolution in 1917, where he used the Military Revolutionary Committee to take over road bridges, telegraph offices and the army headquarters.
- ☑ Trotsky's was appointed as Commissar for War during the Russian Civil War. In this role, he was responsible for the Red Army, and his actions were one of the key reasons the Bolsheviks won.
- ☑ Trotsky negotiated the Treaty of Brest-Litovsk with Germany which was signed on 3rd March, 1918.

What happened to Trotsky during the leadership struggle?

Stalin *(p.64)* managed to remove Trotsky as a rival during the leadership struggle:

- ☑ Trotsky claimed Stalin *(p.64)* deliberately told him the incorrect date for Lenin's funeral. This meant when Trotsky did not attend, his opponents could claim he did not respect Lenin's legacy.
- ☑ In 1924, Stalin *(p.64)* allied with Zinoviev and Kamenev in supporting the New Economic Policy, in order to oppose Trotsky who wanted rapid industrialisation.
- ☑ Zinoviev and Kamenev worked against Trotsky at the Thirteenth Party Congress in 1924, so that all of Trotsky's ideas were rejected.
- ☑ Trotsky lost his job as Commissar for War in 1925.

What happened to Trotsky during the purges?

During the purges:

- ☑ Trotsky was not in the USSR during the Great Purges of 1936 to 1938 as he lived in exile.
- ☑ Other members of the Communist Party were accused of being 'Trotskyites', a threat to the USSR and communicating with Trotsky in their Show Trials.

How did Trotsky die?

Trotsky was murdered in Mexico on 20th August, 1940 by a member of the NKVD *(p.34)* who forced an ice pick into his head.

GENRIKH YAGODA - NKVD

Genrikh Yagoda was the leader of the NKVD when the Great Purge began.

Who was Yagoda?

Genrikh Yagoda joined the Bolshevik Party in 1907. He was a member of the secret police.

When was Yagoda important?

Yagoda was important between 1934 and 1936.

What role did Yagoda have in the Communist Party?

Yagoda's most important role was as head of the secret police or NKVD *(p.34)* from 1934 to 1936 during the Great Purge.

What happened to Yagoda in the Great Purge?

Yagoda was involved in the Great Purge in 2 ways:

- ☑ He organised and led the initial phase of the Great Purge, including the Trial of the Sixteen in 1936, in which Zinoviev and Kamenev were accused of treason and executed.

- ☑ He was arrested and put on trial in the Trial of the Twenty-One in March 1938. He was found guilty of being a member of a Trotskyite conspiracy and sentenced to death.

When did Yagoda die?

Yagoda was executed by being shot on 13th March, 1938.

Quizzes, amazing exam preparation tools and more at GCSEHistory.com

NIKOLAI YEZHOV - NKVD

Nikolai Yezhov was the leader of the NKVD when Great Purge escalated between 1936 and 1938.

Who was Yezhov?

Nikolai Yezhov joined the Communist Party in 1917, was a political commissar in the Red Army during the civil war and replaced Yagoda as the head of the secret police, or NKVD *(p.34)*, in 1936. He was renowned for being vicious and cruel, and he often took part in the torture of the NKVD's victims.

When was Yezhov important?

Yezhov was important during the time of the Great Purge, or Great Terror, between 1936 and 1938.

What was Yezhov's role in the Great Purge?

He was the head of the NKVD *(p.34)* and was responsible for the Great Purge as it escalated and spread to become mass terror. This time period is known as the Yezhovshchina.

Why did Yezhov lose his job?

Stalin *(p.64)* eventually saw Yezhov as suspect and he was arrested and interrogated. He named many of his own family members as suspects which led to hundreds being rounded up and executed.

How did Yezhov die?

He was put on trial, found guilty and executed in February 1940.

DID YOU KNOW?

Yezhov eventually fell from Stalin's favour and was arrested. He confessed to anti-Soviet activity, but later claimed he only did so after being tortured. He was eventually executed in 1940.

GRIGORY ZINOVIEV

Grigory Zinoviev was one of Stalin's opponents in the leadership struggle.

Who was Zinoviev?

Grigory Zinoviev was from a Jewish farming family. He was a member of the Social Democratic Party and became a member of the Bolshevik Party when it was created. He spent time in exile with Lenin before returning to Russia in February 1917.

When did Zinoviev join the Communist Party?

Zinoviev joined the Social Democratic Party in 1901 and became a member of the Bolshevik Party when it was created in 1903.

What was Lenin's relationship with Zinoviev?

Zinoviev was a close friend of Lenin's, but had opposed Lenin's plan for a revolution in October 1917.

What were Zinoviev's political beliefs?

Zinoviev was on the left of the Communist Party. He believed in permanent or world-wide revolution and was against the New Economic Policy, NEP *(p.18)*.

What did Lenin say about Zinoviev in his 'Testament'?

Lenin criticised Zinoviev for not supporting him in the October Revolution of 1917 in his 'Testament'.

What roles did Zinoviev have in the Communist Party?

Zinoviev held 3 key positions of responsibility:

- ☑ In February 1917, Zinoviev was elected chairman of the Council of Commissars of the Petrograd Workers' Commune.
- ☑ In March 1919, he was elected the chairman of the Comintern.
- ☑ From 1921 to 1926, Zinoviev was a full member of the Politburo.

What happened to Zinoviev during the leadership struggle with Stalin?

In 1925, Stalin *(p.64)* allied with Kamenev and Zinoviev to defeat Trotsky. Between 1927 and 1929 Stalin turned against Zinoviev and allied with Bukharin.

What happened to Zinoviev in the Great Purges?

Stalin *(p.64)* viewed Zinoviev as a threat so he was targeted in the Great Purges of 1936 to 1938:

- ☑ He was arrested and put on trial during the Trial of the Sixteen in 1936 with Kamenev.
- ☑ He was accused of the murder of Kirov, plotting to overthrow the government and sabotaging the Five Year Plans.
- ☑ Zinoviev confessed to the crimes of which he was accused to save the lives of his family. He was executed by being shot.

When did Zinoviev die?

Zinoviev was executed after his show trial on 25th August, 1936. He was shot.

DID YOU KNOW?

In 1988, the Soviet government pardoned Zinoviev for the charges that led to his death.

A

Abolish, Abolished - to stop something, or get rid of it.

Agricultural - relating to agriculture.

Agriculture - an umbrella term to do with farming, growing crops or raising animals.

Allegiance - loyalty to a person, group or cause.

Alliance - a union between groups or countries that benefits each member.

Allies - parties working together for a common objective, such as countries involved in a war. In both world wars, 'Allies' refers to those countries on the side of Great Britain.

Ambassador - someone, often a diplomat, who represents their state, country or organisation in a different setting or place.

Assassinate - to murder someone, usually an important figure, often for religious or political reasons.

Assassination - the act of murdering someone, usually an important person.

Autonomy - independence or self-government.

B

Bolshevik, Bolsheviks - was a Russian radical Marxist revolutionary group, founded by Vladimir Lenin and Alexander Bogdanov in 1903. A Bolshevik is someone who is a member of that party.

Bribe, Bribery, Bribes - to dishonestly persuade someone to do something for you in return for money or other inducements.

C

Campaign - a political movement to get something changed; in military terms, it refers to a series of operations to achieve a goal.

Capitalism - the idea of goods and services being exchanged for money, private ownership of property and businesses, and acceptance of a hierarchical society.

Censorship - the control of information in the media by a government, whereby information considered obscene or unacceptable is suppressed.

Civilian - a non-military person.

Claim - someone's assertion of their right to something - for example, a claim to the throne.

Communal - referring to something that is shared by all members of a community, be it an action or possession etc.

Communism - the belief, based on the ideas of Karl Marx, that all people should be equal in society without government, money or private property. Everything is owned by by the people, and each person receives according to need.

Communist - a believer in communism.

Conference - a formal meeting to discuss common issues of interest or concern.

Consolidate - to strengthen a position, often politically, by bringing several things together into a more effective whole.

Constitution - rules, laws or principles that set out how a country is governed.

Consumer goods - products that people buy.

Cooperate, Cooperation - to work together to achieve a common aim. Frequently used in relation to politics, economics or law.

Counter-attack - an attack made in response to one by an opponent.

Culture - the ideas, customs, and social behaviour of a particular people or society.

Currency - an umbrella term for any form of legal tender, but most commonly referring to money.

D

Decree - an official order with the force of law behind it.

Deploy - to move military troops or equipment into position or a place so they are ready for action.

Deport - to expel someone from a country and, usually, return them to their homeland.

Deportation - the act of deporting someone.

Deterrent - something that discourages an action or behaviour.

Dictator - a ruler with absolute power over a country, often acquired by force.

Dictatorship - a form of government where an individual or small group has total power, ruling without tolerance for other views or opposition.

Dictatorship of the Proletariat - the belief that, whilst the proletariat would eventually come to rule itself as proposed by Karl Marx, for now they were not ready, and required a 'dictator' to guide them until they were able to rule themselves.

Discriminate, Discrimination - to treat a person or group of people differently and in an unfair way.

E

Economic - relating to the economy; also used when justifying something in terms of profitability.

Economy - a country, state or region's position in terms of production and consumption of goods and services, and the supply of money.

Encircle, Encirclement - a military term for enemy forces isolating and surrounding their target.

Exile - to be banned from one's original country, usually as a punishment or for political reasons.

Export - to transport goods for sale to another country.

Extreme - furthest from the centre or any given point. If someone holds extreme views, they are not moderate and are considered radical.

F

Famine - a severe food shortage resulting in starvation and death, usually the result of bad harvests.

Front - in war, the area where fighting is taking place.

Full employment - when virtually everyone able and willing to work in a country has a job.

G

Gulag - a forced labour camp in the USSR.

H

Harvest - the process of gathering and collecting crops.

Heavy industry - the manufacture of large and/or heavy items in bulk, or industries which involve large and heavy equipment and/or facilities. Examples are the iron, coal, steel and electricity industries.

Hierarchies, Hierarchy - the ranking of people according to authority, for example a colonel in the army being higher than a corporal.

I

Ideology - a set of ideas and ideals, particularly around political ideas or economic policy, often shared by a group of people.

Illiterate - unable to read or write.

Independence, Independent - to be free of control, often meaning by another country, allowing the people of a nation the ability to govern themselves.

Indoctrinate, Indoctrination - to teach someone to accept a set of beliefs without reservation or question.

Industrial - related to industry, manufacturing and/or production.

Industrialisation, Industrialise, Industrialised - the process of developing industry in a country or region where previously there was little or none.

Industry - the part of the economy concerned with turning raw materials into into manufactured goods, for example making furniture from wood.

Informant - someone who passes important information to another person or organisation, such as the police.

Infrastructure - the basic physical and organisational facilities a society or country needs to function, such as transport networks, communications and power.

K

Kulak - a richer peasant who had sufficient money to own land or a farm.

L

Left wing - used to describe political groups or individuals with beliefs that are usually centered around socialism and the idea of reform.

Legislation - a term for laws when they are considered collectively, for example housing legislation.

Legitimacy, Legitimate - accepted by law or conforming to the rules; can be defended as valid.

Literate - someone who can read and write.

M

Manifesto - the stated policies or aims of a political party or person, normally published before an election.

Military force - the use of armed forces.

Mine - an explosive device usually hidden underground or underwater.

Moderate - someone who is not extreme.

Modernise - to update something to make it suitable for modern times, often by using modern equipment or modern ideas.

Morale - general mood of a group of people.

N

Nationalism, Nationalist, Nationalistic - identifying with your own nation and supporting its interests, often to the detriment or exclusion of other nations.

Nobility - the social class ranked directly below royalty.

O

Occupation - the action, state or period when somewhere is take over and occupied by a military force.

Orthodox - to be normal or usual; to follow or conform to traditional or generally accepted rules or beliefs.

P

POW, Prisoner of war, Prisoners of war - somebody who has been captured and taken prisoner by enemy forces.

Peasant - a poor farmer.

Persecute - to treat someone unfairly because of their race, religion or political beliefs.

Persecution - hostility towards or harassment of someone, usually due to their race, religion or political beliefs.

Pilgrimage - journey undertaken to a sacred place, usually for religious or spiritual reasons.

Poll - a vote or survey.

Population - the number of people who live in a specified place.

Pragmatic - taking a practical approach; being sensible and realistic.

President - the elected head of state of a republic.

Prevent, Preventative, Preventive - steps taken to stop something from happening.

Printing press - a machine that reproduces writing and images by using ink on paper, making many identical copies.

Production - a term used to describe how much of something is made, for example saying a factory has a high production rate.

Profit - generally refers to financial gain; the amount of money made after deducting buying, operating or production costs.

Propaganda - biased information aimed at persuading people to think a certain way.

Purged, Purging - abrupt and often violent removal of a group of people from a place or organisation; medically, to make someone sick or induce diarrhoea as a treatment to rid them of illness.

R

Radical, Radicalism - people who want complete or extensive change, usually politically or socially.

Rationing - limiting goods that are in high demand and short supply.

Real wages - a person's income in terms of how much they can buy after taking inflation into account.

Reconstruction - a period in the USA from 1865-1877 where the southern states were reintegrated through a series of laws.

Republic - a state or country run by elected representatives and an elected/nominated president. There is no monarch.

Revolution - the forced overthrow of a government or social system by its own people.

Right wing - a political view with beliefs centred around nationalism and a desire for an authoritarian government opposed to communism.

S

Sabotage - to deliberately destroy, damage or obstruct, especially to gain a political or military advantage.

Sanitation - conditions relating to public health, such as the sewage system and drinking water supply.

Satellite state - a country under the control of another, such as countries under USSR control during the Cold War.

Scorched earth policy - a military strategy where the retreating forces destroy crops and other resources to prevent the advancing army from using them.

Siege - action by enemy forces to surround a place or building, cutting off access and supplies, with the aim of either destroying it, gaining entry, or starving the inhabitants out.

Socialism - a political and economic system where most resources, such as factories and businesses, are owned by the state or workers with the aim of achieving greater equality between rich and poor.

Socialist - one who believes in the principles of socialism.

Soviet - an elected workers' council at local, regional or national level in the former Soviet Union. It can also be a reference to the Soviet Union or the USSR.

Standard of living - level of wealth and goods available to an individual or group.

State, States - an area of land or a territory ruled by one government.

Strategy - a plan of action outlining how a goal will be achieved.

Strike - a refusal by employees to work as a form of protest, usually to bring about change in their working conditions. It puts pressure on their employer, who cannot run the business without workers.

Successor - someone who succeeds the previous person, such as a leader who takes over the role from the previous holder.

Suppress, Suppression - the use of force to stop something, such as a protest.

T

Tactic - a strategy or method of achieving a goal.

Territories, Territory - an area of land under the control of a ruler/country.

Trade unions - organised groups of workers who cooperate to make their lives better at work. For example, they might negotiate for better pay and then organise a strike if one is refused.

Treason - the crime of betraying one's country, often involving an attempt to overthrow the government or kill the monarch.

Tsar - the Russian word for emperor; can also be spelled 'czar'.

W

Western powers - a group term used to describe developed capitalist nations, such as Britain and the USA.

Working class - socio-economic group consisting of those engaged in waged labour, especially manual work or industry, who typically do not have much money.

A

Art and culture, Soviet Union - *48*

B

Battle of Stalingrad - *56*

C

Censorship in the Soviet Union - *38*

Collectivisation, Soviet Union - *27*

Constitution, Soviet 1936 - *40*

Contenders in the Communist Party leadership struggle - *14*

Cult of Personality - *37*

Cult of Stalin - *37*

E

Education, Soviet Union - *46*

Ethnic minorities, Soviet Union - *51*

F

Family life, Soviet Union - *43*

Family, Soviet Union - *47*

Five Year Plans

the First - *24*

the Fourth - *59*

the Second - *25*

the Third - *26*

Five Year Plans, Soviet Union - *22*

G

Germany, Soviet invasion of - *57*

Gosplan - *23*

Great Retreat - *50*

Gulags - *35*

I

Industrialisation in the Soviet Union - *20*

K

Kamenev, Lev - *60*

Kirov, Sergei - *62*

Kulaks - *30*

L

Leadership struggle in Russia 1924 - 1929 - *16*

Legacy of Stalin - *60*

Lenin, Vladimir - *63*

Living conditions, Soviet Union - *41*

N

Nazi invasion of USSR - *53*

Nazi-Soviet Pact - *52*

New Economic Policy (NEP) - *18*

P

Propaganda in the Soviet Union - *38*

Purges, Soviet Union - *31*

R

Religion, communist views - *49*

S

STALIN - *64*

Second World War, impact on Soviet Union - *58*

Secret Police, Soviet - *34*

Socialist realism - *39*

Soviet invasion of Germany - *57*

Stakhanovite movement - *26*

Stalin as a leader - *55*

Stalingrad, Battle of - *56*

T

Trotsky, Leon - *67*

W

Women, Soviet Union - *44*

Working conditions, Soviet Union - *42*

Y

Yagoda, Genrikh - *68*

Yezhov, Nikolai - *69*

Z

Zinoviev, Grigory - *69*

Quizzes, amazing exam preparation tools and more at GCSEHistory.com